Uncommon Beauty

Wildflowers and Flowering Shrubs
of Southern Alberta and
Southeastern British Columbia

Neil L. Jennings

VICTORIA CALGARY VANCOUVER

Rocky Mountain Books
#108 – 17665 66A Avenue
Surrey, BC V3S 2A7
www.rmbooks.com

Library and Archives Canada Cataloguing in Publication

Jennings, Neil L
Uncommon beauty : wildflowers and flowering shrubs of southern Alberta and southeastern British Columbia / Neil L. Jennings.

Includes bibliographical references and index.
ISBN 1-894765-75-3

1. Wild flowers—Alberta—Identification. 2. Wild flowers—British Columbia—Kootenay Region—Indentification. I. Title.

QK203.W47J46 2006   582.13'097123'4   C2006-900379-3

Edited by SKB
Proofread by Corina Skavberg
Book design by John Luckhurst GDL
Cover design by John Luckhurst GDL
All cover and interior photographs provided by Neil L. Jennings

Printed in China
1 2 3 4 5 6 7 8/11 10 09 07 06

Rocky Mountain Books acknowledges the financial support for its publishing program from the Government of Canada through the Book Publishing Industry Development Program (BPIDP).

ACKNOWLEDGEMENTS

I owe a debt of gratitude to a number of family members and friends who contributed to this book by their continuous encouragement and support. Particular appreciation goes to my wife, Linda, who accompanied me on many flower outings, and allowed me frequent absences from other duties in favour of chasing blooming flowers. My son Shawn, his wife Stacy, my daughter Jenise, her husband Chris, my son Matthew, my son Simon, and his bride Tina, all deserve mention as well, given that they were often seconded to tramp around with me. Thanks also go to my friends Dennis Hall, Homer Spencer, Elizabeth Spencer, Mike Gifford, Russ Webb, and Judy McPhee, who encouraged me in this project and often went into the field with me, according me a level of patience that was above and beyond the call of duty. I also wish to especially thank (or perhaps blame) Don Cahoon, who shamed me with my ignorance and convinced me to educate myself about the Uncommon Beauty that resides in our area.

For Linda, with thanks for your support and patience.

CONTENTS

INTRODUCTION

This book is intended to be a guide for the non-botanist to the identification of wild, flowering plants commonly found in southern Alberta and southeastern British Columbia. I am not a botanist and I have had no formal training in that field of science. I am, however, curious, and I spend a lot of time outdoors with a camera and a fly rod. I have always found wildflowers fascinating in their uncommon beauty, intricacy, and complexity, and recognizing the wildflowers that I encounter enhances my enjoyment in the field. I believe that most people will enjoy a richer experience outdoors if they likewise recognize the wildflowers they discover. It is not terribly difficult to do. Stop and consider that you can easily put names and faces together for several hundred friends, acquaintances, movie stars, authors, business and world leaders, sports figures, etc. Wildflower recognition does not differ from that, and it need not be complicated.

I own a number of wildflower guidebooks and have consulted them extensively over the years, even to the point of having some of them unravel at the binding and fall to pieces. As much as I have used such books, it has always occurred to me that they all share a couple of deficiencies for the non-botanist. Firstly, the photographs in the books are usually too small and/or they lack the detail necessary to make identification easy, or even possible, in some cases. Secondly, the books are written by botanists and assume a level of botanical expertise in the reader that does not exist. In my view, what most people really want to know about wildflowers is "what is this thing?" and "tell me something interesting about it." Botanical detail, while intriguing and enlightening to some of us, will turn off many people.

So I have set out to produce the best photographic representations I could, together with some information about the plant that the reader might find interesting and that might assist the reader in remembering the names of the plants. This is not a book for scientists. It is a book for the curious. There is only a minimal amount of technical jargon herein. I have considered all of the entries to be wildflowers, while realizing that, strictly speaking, some of the inclusions are really shrubs. What I am attempting to do is assist people who want to be able to recognize and identify common wildflowers that they see while outdoors. I have tried to keep it simple and useful, yet interesting.

The wildflowers depicted in the book are arranged first by colour, and then by family. This is a logical arrangement for the non-botanist because the first thing a person notes about a flower is its colour. All of the flowers shown in the book are identified by their prevailing common names used in southern Alberta and southeastern British Columbia. Where I knew of other common names applied to any wildflower, I noted them. I have also included the scientific names of the flowers. This inclusion is made to promote specificity. Common names vary significantly from one geographic area to another; scientific names do not. For example, the common names for Calypso bulbosa, an early-blooming orchid of the Rocky Mountains, include 'Fairy Slipper,' 'Venus Slipper,' 'Cytherea,' 'Deer-head Orchid,' 'Hider of the North,' 'Pink Slipper,' 'Lady's Slipper,' 'False Lady's Slipper,' and probably several more of which I am unaware. If you want to learn the scientific names of the plants to promote precision, fine. If you do not want to deal with that, fine. Just be mindful that many plants have different common names depending on geography and local usage.

This is not a complete guide to all of the wildflowers found in southern Alberta and southeastern British Columbia. What is included here is a collection of some of the more common flowering plants in the region— plants that any one of us could encounter any particular day in season.

A few cautionary comments and suggestions:

While you are outdoors, walk carefully among the plants so as not to damage or disturb them. In parks, stay on the established trails.

Do not pick the flowers. Leave them for others to enjoy. Bear in mind that in national and provincial parks it is illegal to pick any flowers.

Do not eat any plants or plant parts. To do so presents a potentially significant health hazard. Some plants are poisonous.

Do not attempt to use any plants or plant parts for medicinal purposes. To do so presents a potentially significant health hazard. Some plants are poisonous.

One final cautionary note—the pursuit of wildflowers can be addictive, though not hazardous to your health.

Neil L. Jennings
Calgary, Alberta

PLANT SHAPES AND FORMS

Parts of a Leaf

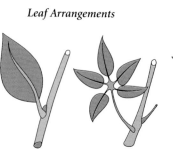

vein
midrib
blade
node
petiole

Parts of a Flower

stamen { filament, anther
petal
sepal
stigma
style
ovary } pistil
receptacle
pedicel

Leaf Arrangements

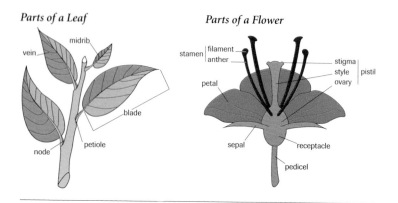

simple   compound – palmate   compound – pinnate   compound – doubly pinnate

---

Stem Arrangements

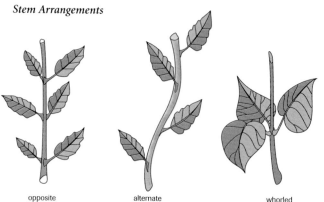

opposite   alternate   whorled

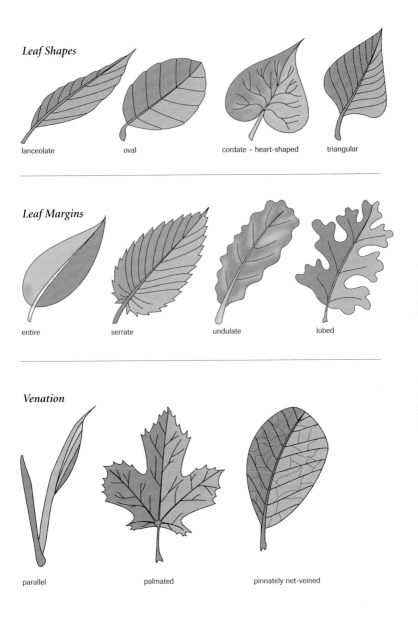

Leaf Shapes

lanceolate   oval   cordate – heart-shaped   triangular

Leaf Margins

entire   serrate   undulate   lobed

Venation

parallel   palmated   pinnately net-veined

TERRITORIAL RANGE OF WILDFLOWERS

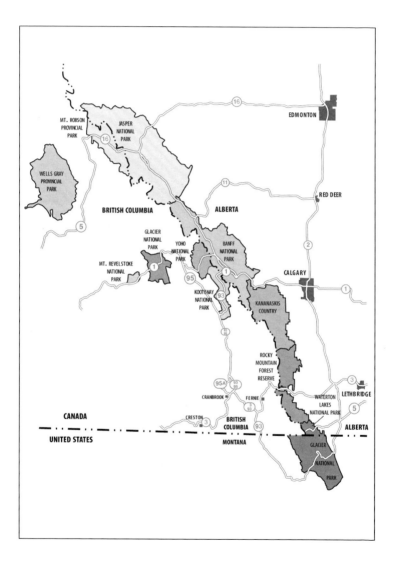

Yellow Flowers

This section includes flowers that are
predominantly yellow when encountered in
the field. The colour varies from bright yellow to
pale cream. Some of the flowers that could appear
in this yellow section have other colour variations,
and you might have to check other sections of
the book to find the flower. For example, the
Paintbrushes (*Castilleja* sp) have a yellow
variation, but they are most often encountered
in a red colour, and they have been pictured
in that section for purposes of sorting.

Oregon Grapes

Mahonia repens (LINDL.) G. DON (ALSO *Berberis repens* LINDL.)

BARBERRY FAMILY

This evergreen plant is widespread and common at low to mid elevations in dry plateaus and dry to moist forests and openings in the foothills. A low-growing shrub that very closely resembles holly, with shiny, sharp-pointed leaves that turn to lovely orange and rusty colours in the fall. The flowers are yellow and bloom in the early spring, giving way to a small, purple berry that resembles a grape.

The fruits are very bitter tasting from the plant, but make a delicious jelly. Native peoples extracted a bright yellow pigment from the inner bark and roots of the plant and used it to dye basket material. The inner bark was also used for medicinal purposes, including easing child delivery, healing wounds, combatting infections, and treating venereal disease.

Puccoon (Lemonweed)
Lithospermum ruderale DOUGL. EX LEHM.

BORAGE FAMILY

A coarse perennial up to 50 cm high, this plant is firmly anchored to dry slopes and grasslands by a large, woody taproot. The numerous leaves are sharp-pointed and lance-shaped, and clasp the stem. The small, yellow flowers are partly hidden in the axils of the leaves near the top of the plant and have a strong, pleasant scent. The stems and leaves are covered in long, white hairs. The fruit is an oval, cream-coloured nutlet that is somewhat pitted and resembles pointed teeth.

The genus name, *Lithospermum*, comes from the Greek *lithos*, meaning "stone," and *sperma*, meaning "seed," a reference to the fruit of the plant. Indeed, another common name for the plant is Stoneseed. For centuries some Native peoples used an extract of the plant for birth control. Natural estrogens in the plant suppress the release of certain hormones required for ovulation. The roots of the plant were used as a source of red dye.

Yellow Buckwheat (Umbrella Plant)

Eriogonum flavum NUTT.

BUCKWHEAT FAMILY

This fuzzy-haired, tufted perennial favours dry, often sandy or rocky outcrops, eroded slopes, and badlands. The leaves are dark green on top, but appear white and felty on the underside due to the dense hairs. The yellow flowers occur in compound umbels—umbrella-shaped clusters—atop the stem. The common name for the plant, Umbrella Plant, is testimony to the shape of the florescence.

The genus name, *Eriogonum*, comes from the Greek *erion*, meaning "wool," and *gony*, meaning "knee" or "joint." *Flavum* means "yellow." The plant has an unpleasant smell, but the nectar is relished by bees and produces a strongly flavoured, buckwheat-like honey.

Marsh Marigold
Caltha palustris L.

BUTTERCUP FAMILY

Favouring wet meadows, woods, and bogs, the Marsh Marigold is often found in the shallow water of slow-moving streams and ditches. The flower has five to nine bright yellow, showy sepals, but no petals. The leaves are mostly basal and quite distinctive, being dark green, large, and round to kidney- or heart-shaped.

The common name is said to have come from Mary's Gold, a reference to a yellow flower esteemed by the Virgin Mary. The plant is not a true marigold. True marigolds belong to the Aster family. The genus name, *Caltha*, is derived from the Greek word *kalathos*, meaning "goblet." The species name, *palustris*, is Latin meaning "of marshes or wet places." All parts of the mature plant are poisonous, but they are said to be distasteful to livestock because of the acrid juice.

Sagebrush Buttercup
Ranunculus glaberrimus HOOK.
BUTTERCUP FAMILY

This beautiful little buttercup is one of the earliest blooming wildflowers, with its bright yellow, shiny petals. The bright flowers peep out from the dead winter grasses of early spring on arid hillsides. The leaves are mainly basal and elliptic to lance-shaped. The flowers appear in patches or as single blooms.

Buttercups are among the oldest of flower families, existing for millions of years before earliest humans developed, and are considered one of the most primitive plant families. The cell structure on the petals is such that there is air in the cell-vacuoles, and this is responsible for the 'whiteness' seen on the petals. The genus name, *Ranunculus*, comes from the Greek *rana*, which means "frog," a likely reference to the wetland or marshy habitat of many species of the family. The species name, *glaberrimus*, means "very smooth" or "smoothest," most probably a reference to the shiny, hairless leaves. Sagebrush Buttercups are poisonous, containing an acrid alkaloid, and some Native tribes warned their children not to touch or pick them. Some Native people used the flower as a source of poison for their arrows.

Creeping Buttercup
Ranunculus cymbalaria PURSH
BUTTERCUP FAMILY

This Buttercup spreads over the ground by slender, creeping stems or runners, similar to those of the Wild Strawberry. The leaf blades are long-stalked and egg- or heart-shaped, and have scalloped margins. The plant is found in moist meadows, on streambanks, and at the margins of lakes and ponds.

The genus name, *Ranunculus*, is explained in the note on Sagebrush Buttercup, above. The species name, *cymbalaria*, means "pertaining to cymbals" and is most probably a reference to the shape of the leaves.

Meadow Buttercup
Ranunculus acris L.
BUTTERCUP FAMILY

Among the tallest of the Buttercups, this plant may reach almost a metre in height. It is a hairy perennial, with broad, five-sided leaves that are deeply lobed and divided nearly to the base. The flowers are glossy yellow, with greenish, hairy sepals that fall off soon after the flower blooms.

The species name, *acris*, means "acrid" and refers to the juice of this plant.

Yellow Columbine

Aquilegia flavescens WATS.

BUTTERCUP FAMILY

Lemon yellow in colour, these beautiful flowers nod at the ends of slender stems that lift the flowers above the leaves. Each flower is composed of five wing-shaped sepals and five tube-shaped petals that flare at the open end and taper to a distinctive spur at the opposite end. The plant occurs in the alpine and subalpine zones.

The origin of the genus name, *Aquilegia*, is the subject of some debate. One school holds that it is derived from the Latin, *aquila*, meaning "eagle," and refers to the long, talon-like spur on the flower. Another school argues that the genus name is from *aqua*, meaning "water," and *legere*, meaning "collect," a reference to the drops of nectar that collect at the end of the spur. The common name, Columbine, is derived from *columba*, meaning "dove," it being said that the petals resemble a group of doves. Bumblebees and butterflies favour Columbines. In addition to the yellow variety, Columbines are also found in the region in blue (*A. brevistyla*) and red (*A. formosa*).

Heart-Leaved Alexanders (Meadow Parsnip)

Zizia aptera, (A. GRAY) FERN.

CARROT FAMILY

A plant of prairies, moist meadows, open woods, streambanks, and wetland margins. The small, bright yellow flowers are numerous, and occur in compound, flat-topped clusters at the top of the stems. The lower leaves are leathery, dark green, and heart-shaped. The stem leaves are smaller and divided into three leaflets. The stem leaves become progressively smaller along the stem until they become cleft leaflets. The flowers appear on top of hollow stems that are erect and reach heights of up to 60 cm.

The origin of the name Alexanders is unknown. The genus name, *Zizia*, honours an early German botanist, Johann Baptist Ziz. The species name, *aptera*, means "wingless," probably a reference to the shape of the fruit of the plant.

Narrow-Leaved Desert Parsley (Nine-Leaf Biscuit-Root)
Lomatium triternatum (PURSH) COULT. AND ROSE

CARROT FAMILY

This perennial herb occurs in dry to moist open sites, and in foothills to montane elevations, and grows to 80 cm in height. The leaves are mostly basal, hairy, and divided into segments—often in three sets of three leaflets each. The stalks are irregular in length and clasp the stem. The flowers are very small and yellow, occurring in compound, flat-topped clusters (umbels) atop the stalks. Often there are a few slender, leafy bracts just below the junction of the individual stalks, but no bracts occur at the base of the flower arrangement.

Native peoples made extensive use of the plant as a food source. The species name, *triternatum*, means "divided three times in threes," a reference to the leaf construction. The Lewis and Clark expedition journals describe how the Natives ground the roots of the plant into a meal or flour that was then shaped into flat cakes, thus the source for another common name, Nine-Leaf Biscuit-Root. A specimen of the plant was collected by the expedition in Idaho in 1806 and was later described by Frederick Pursh.

Annual Hawk's-Beard

Crepis tectorum (JAMES) T. AND G.

COMPOSITE FAMILY

A plant of moist, open areas and saline meadows, this one- to three-stemmed annual will grow up to a metre in height. The basal leaves usually wither before flowering occurs. The stems have a few thin alternate leaves. Each plant will produce a few to 15 yellow flowers, composed of yellow ray flowers and no disk flowers. The fruits of the plant are dark purplish-brown achenes with a pappus of fine, white, hair-like bristles at the top.

The genus name, *Crepis*, is derived from the Greek *krepis*, meaning "boot" or "sandal," and it may refer to the deeply cut leaves, which may suggest the thongs of a sandal. The name Hawk's-Beard was given to the genus *Crepis* by the botanist Asa Grey, and it might refer to the pappus's resemblance to the bristly feathers that surround a hawk's beak.

Arrow-Leaved Balsamroot

Balsamorhiza sagittata (PURCH) NUTT.

COMPOSITE FAMILY

A widespread and frequently abundant plant of hot, arid climates, often found on rocky, south-facing slopes. The flowers are solitary composite heads with bright yellow ray flowers and yellow disk flowers, densely hairy, especially at the base. The leaves are large, arrowhead-shaped, silvery in colour, and covered by dense, felt-like hairs.

Also known as Oregon Sunflowers, the Arrow-Leaved Balsamroot often provides a showy, early spring splash of colour on warm, dry hillsides. All parts of the plant are edible and provided an important food source for Native peoples. Some tribes smoked the leaves like tobacco. The seeds are similar to sunflower seeds and were often dried and ground for use as flour. Deer and elk commonly browse on the plants. The genus name, *Balsamorhiza*, comes from the Greek *balsamon*, meaning "balsam," and *rhiza*, meaning "root," referring to the aromatic resin of the taproot.

Arrow-Leaved Groundsel (Giant Ragwort)
Senecia triangularis HOOK.

COMPOSITE FAMILY

This tall (up to 1.5 m), leafy, lush perennial herb often grows in large clumps in moist to wet, open or partly shaded sites in the foothills to the alpine elevations. The leaves are alternate, spearhead- or arrowhead-shaped, squared off at the base, and tapered to the point. The leaves are numerous and well developed along the whole stem of the plant. They are widest near the middle of the stem and are coarsely sharp-toothed. The flowers occur in flat-topped clusters at the top of the plant and have five to eight bright yellow ray florets surrounding a disk of bright yellow to orange florets.

The species name, *triangularis*, refers to the shape of the leaves, a distinguishing feature of the plant. The common name, Ragwort, is said to refer to the ragged appearance of the leaf margins in many members of the genus. Many members of the genus contain poisonous alkaloids, but livestock seem to find the plants unpalatable.

Brown-Eyed Susan
Gaillardia aristata PURSH

COMPOSITE FAMILY

A plant of open grasslands, dry hillsides, roadsides, and open woods. The flowers are large and showy, with yellow ray florets that are purplish to reddish at the base. The central disk is purplish and woolly-hairy. The leaves are numerous, alternate, and lance-shaped, usually looking greyish and rough owing to the many short hairs.

The plant is named after a French botanist, Gaillard de Marentonneau. The species name, *aristata*, means "bristly" or "bearded," a reference to the bristles on the flower head. A number of Native peoples used the plant for medicinal purposes, relieving a variety of ailments from menstrual problems, gastroenteritis, and venereal disease, to saddle sores on horses. This flower is also commonly known as Blanketflower. The plant was first named and described by Frederick Pursh in 1814 from a specimen collected by Meriwether Lewis in 1806.

Common Dandelion
Taraxacum officinale WEBER.

COMPOSITE FAMILY

This common, introduced plant is found in a variety of habitats the world over, and it is probably the most recognizable flower in our area for most people. The bright yellow flowers have ray florets only and appear at the top of a smooth stem that arises from a whorl of basal leaves that are lance- to spoon-shaped and deeply incised. The flowers appear from early in the spring until late in the fall, giving this plant undoubtedly the longest blooming time of any flower in our area.

Though everybody seems to recognize this flower, it is interesting to note that more than 1,000 kinds of Dandelions have been described. The common name for this plant is thought to be a corruption of the French *le dent-de-lion*, meaning "the tooth of the lion," a reference to the shape of the leaf. All parts of the plant are edible—the young leaves are eaten raw or cooked as greens, the roots are dried and ground as a coffee substitute, and the flowers can be used to make wine. Some people roll the flower heads in flour and deep-fry them, claiming that they have a flavour similar to morel mushrooms when so prepared. The sap from the plant was used in Ireland to treat warts.

Common Tansy
Tanacetum vulgare L.

COMPOSITE FAMILY

This plant was introduced from Europe and is common along roadsides, embankments, pastures, fencerows, and disturbed areas. The flowers are yellow and occur in numerous bunches atop multiple stalks. They are flattened and resemble yellow buttons. The leaves are almost fern-like, dark green, finely dissected, and strong smelling.

Tansies are also known as Button Flowers. The genus name, *Tanacetum*, comes from the Greek word *athanatos*, meaning "long-lasting," possibly a reference to the long-lasting flowers. In England the plant was placed in shrouds to repel insects and rodents from corpses. It was originally cultivated in North America for its medicinal properties, and it spread from those cultivations. During the Middle Ages a posy of Tansies was thought to ward off the Black Death.

Goat's-Beard
Tragopogon dubius SCOP.

COMPOSITE FAMILY

A plant of the grasslands, roadsides, ditches, and dry waste areas. Goat's-Beard was introduced from Europe and is also known as "Yellow Salsify." The flower is a large, solitary, erect yellow head, surrounded by long, narrow, green, protruding bracts. The leaves are alternate, fleshy, and narrow, but broad and clasping at the base. The fruit is a mass of white, narrow, ribbed, beaked achenes that resembles the seed pod of a common dandelion, but is significantly larger—approaching the size of a softball.

The flowers open on sunny mornings, but then close up around noon and stay closed for the rest of the day. They usually will not open on cloudy or rainy days. The common name, Goat's-Beard, is probably a reference to the mass of white achenes, which is said to resemble a goat's beard. The genus name, *Tragopogon*, is derived from the Greek *tragos*, meaning "goat," and *pogon*, meaning "beard." The young leaves and roots from immature plants may be eaten. The leaves and stems exude a milky, latex-like juice when cut, which may be chewed like gum when hardened. A similar species, Purple Salsify or Oyster Plant (*T. porrifolius*), appears in the same habitat, but has a purple flower.

Hairy Golden Aster

Heterotheca villosa (PURSH) SHINNERS

COMPOSITE FAMILY

This is a plant of dry, open, sandy prairie and hillsides, particularly where there are southerly exposures. The bright yellow flowers appear in numbers, with bright yellow ray florets and yellow to brown disk florets. The leaves are oblong and more or less hairy.

The species name, *villosa*, means "hairy" and refers to the overall hairiness of the plant. At one time this plant had the scientific name *Chrysopsis villosa*. *Chrysopsis* is from the Greek *chrysos*, meaning "gold" and *opsis*, meaning "aspect"—thus Golden Aster.

Heart-Leafed Arnica
Arnica cordifolia HOOK.

COMPOSITE FAMILY

A plant of the wooded areas in the Rocky Mountains and of the foothills and boreal forest. The leaves occur in two to four opposite pairs along the stem, each with a long stalk and heart-shaped, serrated blade. The uppermost pair are stalkless and more lance-shaped than the lower leaves. The flowers have 10–15 bright yellow ray florets and bright yellow central disk florets.

Without careful dissection of the plant and examination under magnification, recognition of specific members of the *Arnica* family can be difficult. The leaf structure on an individual plant is often the best clue to species recognition. The genus name, *Arnica*, is rooted in the Greek *arnakis*, meaning "lamb's skin," a reference to the woolly bracts and leaf texture on many members of the genus. The species name, *cordifolia*, means "heart-shaped," a reference to the leaves of the plant. This species occasionally hybridizes with Mountain Arnica (*A. latifolia*), and the resulting hybrid can be difficult to identify. A number of Native peoples used Arnicas as a poultice for swellings and bruises. Arnicas are said to be poisonous if ingested.

Late Goldenrod

Solidago gigantea AIT. SSP. SEROTINA (AIT.) MCNEILL

COMPOSITE FAMILY

A plant of moist woods and meadows, floodplains, and lake shores. The flowers are bright yellow clusters of terminal, broadly pyramidal clusters of flower heads. The leaves are numerous, alternate, thin, and lance-shaped, tapering to the base.

The genus name, *Solidago*, is probably from the Latin *solidus*, meaning "whole," and *ago*, meaning "to do or make," because of the plant's healing properties. Some Native peoples ground the flowers into a lotion and applied it to bee stings.

Perennial Sow Thistle
Sonchus arvensis L.

COMPOSITE FAMILY

A plant of cultivated fields, roadsides, ditches, and pastures. The flowers have large yellow ray florets similar to dandelion flowers. Sow Thistle is an imported species from Europe. It is not a true thistle. Sow Thistles will exude a milky latex when the stem is crushed. True thistles do not do so.

The common name is derived from the fact that pigs like to eat this plant. The genus name, *Sonchus*, is from the Greek word *somphos*, meaning "spongy," a reference to the stems. The species name, *arvensis*, means "of the fields," a reference to the fact that the plant often invades cultivated ground.

Pineapple Weed
Matricaria discoidea DC

COMPOSITE FAMILY

This branching annual grows up to 40 cm tall along roadsides, in ditches, and on disturbed ground. The stem leaves are alternate and fern-like, with finely dissected narrow segments. Basal leaves have usually fallen off before flowering occurs. The flowers are several to many composite heads with greenish to yellow disk florets on a cone-shaped or dome-shaped base. There are no ray florets.

The genus name, *Matricaria*, is from the Latin *mater* or *matrix*, meaning "mother" or "womb," and *caria*, meaning "dear," and is a reference to use of the plant in the treatment of uterine infections and other gynecological conditions. When crushed, the leaves and flowers of the plant produce a distinctive pineapple aroma, hence the common name. Some Native peoples used the plant medicinally, while others used the plant to scent their homes and baby cradles or as an insect repellant. Meriwether Lewis collected a sample of the plant in 1806 while he stayed with the Nez Perce Indians in Idaho. The plant is also known as Rayless Chamomile. Wild Chamomile (*M. recutita*) has similar leaves to Pineapple Weed, but its flowers resemble Ox-Eye Daisy. Wild Chamomile has been used by herbalists for treatment of a variety of conditions.

Prairie Coneflower
Ratibida columnifera (NUTT.) WOOTON AND STANDL.

COMPOSITE FAMILY

This is a plant of dry grasslands, coulees, and disturbed areas, and can reach heights of up to 60 cm. The leaves are alternate, grayish-green in colour, and deeply divided into oblong lobes. The distinctive flower appears atop a tall, slender stem, and consists of dark purple disk florets formed into a cylinder up to 4 cm long, the base of which is surrounded by bright yellow petals.

The origin of the genus name, *Ratibida*, is unknown. The species name, *columnifera*, refers to the column- or cone-shaped flower. Some Native peoples dried the flowers for food, while others made a tea from the disk florets and leaves. The roots of the plant yield a yellow dye.

Prairie Groundsel

Senecio canus HOOK.

COMPOSITE FAMILY

This is a white, woolly perennial that can stand up to 40 cm in height.
It occurs at a variety of elevations, from prairie to almost timberline.
The leaves are clustered at the base, with taller stems supporting the flowers.
Stem leaves are alternate and reduced in size as the stem rises. All leaves are
greyish green, and covered with white, fuzzy hairs. The yellow flower heads
are solitary to several on a stem, with notched ray florets surrounding a
cluster of disk florets.

The genus name, *Senecio*, is from the Latin *senex*, meaning "old man,"
and may be a reference to the grey, beard-like hair that covers the plant.
The species name, *canus*, means "ash-coloured," and refers to the leaves.
The Groundsels contain toxic alkaloids. Other common names applied
to plants in this genus include Butterweed and Ragwort.

Prickly Lettuce
Lactuca serriola L. (ALSO *L. scariola*)
COMPOSITE FAMILY

This plant grows in fields and disturbed areas at low to mid elevations. The leaves are once or twice lobed and prickly on the sides. The flowers have composite heads, with yellow ray flowers and no disk flowers.

Prickly Lettuce is an introduced species, having come from Europe. It has become an invasive weed in many areas of North America. It is a close relative of Common Blue Lettuce (*L. tatarica*). Both plants will exude a milky sap when the stem is broken, *lac* being Latin for "milk," hence the genus name. Both of the species names—*serriola* and *scariola*—are alternative spellings and both mean "of salads." In fact, garden lettuce is a member of this genus.

Shining Arnica (Orange Arnica)
Arnica fulgens PURSH
COMPOSITE FAMILY

A plant of moist grasslands to low elevations in the mountains, this Arnica grows up to 60 cm in height. The leaves are greyish-green and mostly basal, opposite, lance-shaped, stalked, and tapering to the base. There are small tufts of brown hairs between the basal leaf stalks and stem. The paired stem leaves are smaller than the basal leaves, stalkless, or nearly so, and lance-shaped to linear. The flower heads are usually solitary with yellow ray florets surrounding yellow disk florets that exhibit spreading white hairs.

For an explanation of the genus name, see Heart-Leaved Arnica. The species name, *fulgens,* means "shining," and is said to refer to the bright flowers against the greyish-green background of the plant's leaves. This species occasionally hybridizes with Mountain Arnica (*A. latifolia*), and the resulting hybrid can be difficult to identify. A number of Native peoples used Arnicas as a poultice for swellings and bruises. Arnicas are said to be poisonous if ingested.

Short-Beaked Agoseris (False Dandelion)

Agoseris glauca (PURSH) RAF.

COMPOSITE FAMILY

A plant common to moist-to-dry meadows and dry, open forests.
This plant is also known as False Dandelion. The Agoseris shares many characteristics with the Dandelions, including a long taproot, rosette of basal leaves, a leafless stem, a single yellow flower appearing on a long stalk, and the production of a sticky, milky juice which is apparent when the stem is broken. In fact, this flower is often passed over as just another Dandelion, but upon closer examination several differences are apparent. Agoseris is generally a taller plant than Dandelion, its leaves are longer, and the leaf blades are smooth or faintly toothed, rather than deeply incised. The bracts of the Agoseris flower heads are broader than Dandelions, and are never turned back along the stem, as they are in Dandelions.

Some Native peoples used the milky juice of the plant as a chewing gum. Infusions from the plant were also used for a variety of medicinal purposes. Agoseris also appears in an orange form (*A. aurantiaca*) that inhabits the same environment.

Slender Hawkweed

Hieracium gracile L.

COMPOSITE FAMILY

A plant common to open woods, meadows, roadsides, ditches, and disturbed areas. The yellow flower heads appear in a cluster on ascending stalks. The flowers are composed entirely of ray florets, no disk florets. The leaves are in a basal rosette, broadly lanced to spoon-shaped.

The genus name *Hieracium* comes from the Greek *hierax*, meaning "hawk," as it was once believed that eating these plants improved a hawk's vision. The species name, *gracile*, means "slender." The leaves, stems, and roots produce a milky latex that was used as a chewing gum by British Columbia tribes. A similar species, Orange Hawkweed (*H. aurantiacum*), occurs in similar habitat.

Spikelike Goldenrod

Solidago simplex DC. (ALSO *S. spathulata* AND *S. decumbens*)

COMPOSITE FAMILY

This plant occurs at low to alpine elevations in dry areas, forest openings, and meadows. It can grow to heights of up to 80 cm and has broadly lanced to spoon-shaped leaves that have hairless toothed edges. The flowers occur in a dense, narrow, elongated cluster or raceme.

It is a popular misconception that Goldenrods cause hayfever, but in fact, the pollen of the Goldenrods is too heavy to be easily carried on the wind —it must be carried from flower to flower by insects.

Yellow Evening Primrose
Oenothera biennis L.

EVENING PRIMROSE FAMILY

An erect, robust, leafy biennial, this plant forms a rosette of leaves the first year and puts up a tall, leafy stem the second. The flowers have large, bright yellow, cross-shaped stigma, with numerous yellow stamens. The flowers usually open in the evening and fade in the morning.

The plant gets it common name by its habit of blooming at dusk to attract moths for pollination. The genus name, *Oenothera,* is from a Greek work meaning "wine-scented"—*oinos* meaning "wine" and *thera* meaning "to induce wine drinking." The roots of the first-year plant were often dug and boiled for food, or were dried for later use. They are said to be nutritious and have a nut-like flavour. Seed oil from the plant is used for medicinal purposes.

Butter and Eggs
Linaria vulgares P. MILL

FIGWORT FAMILY

A common plant of roadsides, ditches, fields, and disturbed areas that reaches heights of up to a metre. Also known as Toadflax. The leaves are alternate, dark green, and narrow. The flowers are similar in shape to Snapdragons. The bright yellow flowers with orange throats occur in dense, terminal clusters at the tops of erect stems. The corolla is spurred at the base and two-lipped: the upper lip two-lobed and the lower lip three-lobed.

The flower takes its common name, Butter and Eggs, from the yellow and orange tones that resemble the colour of butter and eggs. There are two schools of thought as to the origin of the other common name, Toadflax. In early English, "toad" meant "false" or "useless," ergo "useless flax" or "false flax"—the leaves of this plant resembling those of Flax. The other school of thought attributes the name "toad" to the resemblance of the flower to that of a toad's mouth. Toadflax was introduced to North America from Europe as a garden plant, but escapees from the garden have become noxious weeds. It was used in early Europe to treat jaundice, piles, and eye infections, and was also boiled in milk to make a fly poison. The genus name, *Linaria*, refers to the general similarity of the leaves of this plant to those of Flax. Dalmatian Toadflax (*L. dalmatica*) is a similar species that appears in the same habitat. It has clasping, broadly oval leaves and larger flowers.

Mullein

Verbascum thapsus L.

FIGWORT FAMILY

A Eurasian import that grows up to two metres tall, Mullein is quite common along roadsides, gravelly places, and dry slopes. The plant is a biennial, taking two years to produce flowers. In the first year the plant puts out a rosette of large leaves that are very soft to the touch, much like velvet or flannel. From those leaves surges the strong, sentinel-like stalk in the second year. The small, yellow flowers appear randomly from a flowering spike atop the stalk. It appears that at no time do all the flowers bloom together. After flowering, the dead stalk turns to dark brown and the stalk may persist for many months.

A common name for the plant is Flannel Mullein, a reference to the soft texture of the basal leaves. Mullein is from the Latin *mollis*, which means "soft." The dried leaves of the plant were sometimes smoked by Native peoples, and the plant is also sometimes called Indian Tobacco. The crushed leaves were often used as a poultice and applied to swelling and wounds because the chemicals in the plant soothe irritated tissues and act as a sedative.

Yellow Beardtongue

Penstemon confertus DOUGL.

FIGWORT FAMILY

A plant of moist to dry meadows, woodlands, streambanks, hillsides, and mountains. The small, pale yellow flowers are numerous and appear in whorled, interrupted clusters along the upper part of the stem. Each flower is tube-shaped, and has two lips. The lower lip is three-lobed and bearded at the throat; the upper lip is two-lobed.

The common name, Beardtongue, describes the hairy, tongue-like staminode (sterile stamen) in the throat of the flower. The genus name, *Penstemon*, originates from the Greek *pente*, meaning "five," and *stemon*, meaning "stamen," five being the total number of stamens in the flower. The species name, *confertus*, is Latin, meaning "crowded," a reference to the numerous flowers in the clusters. A number of Penstemons appear in Western Canada.

Yellow Monkeyflower

Mimulus guttatus FISCH. EX DC.

FIGWORT FAMILY

This plant occurs, often in large patches, along streams, seeps, and in moist meadows. The plant is quite variable, but always spectacular when found. The bright yellow flowers resemble Snapdragons and occur in clusters. The flowers usually have red or purple dots on the lip, giving the appearance of a grinning face.

The genus name, *Mimulus*, is from the Latin *mimus*, meaning "mimic" or "actor," a reference to the face seen on the flower. The species name, *guttatus*, means "spotted" or "speckled." A related species, Red Monkeyflower (*M. lewisii*), is named in honour of Meriwether Lewis of the Lewis and Clark expedition, who collected the first specimen of the plant in 1805 near the headwaters of the Missouri River in Montana.

Yellow Owl's Clover
Orthocarpus luteus NUTT.

FIGWORT FAMILY

This plant thrives in dry soils, open woodlands, and sagebrush communities. It bears a strong resemblance to Paintbrushes (*Castilleja* spp.), but Owl's Clover is an annual and both lips of the flower tube are about equal length.

The genus name, *Orthocarpus*, is from the Greek *orthos*, meaning "straight," and *karpos* meaning "fruit," a reference to the straight seed capsule of the plant. The botanist Thomas Nuttall collected and described the first specimen of Owl's Clover in the early 1800s when he travelled up the Missouri River with the American Fur Company. The plant was used by some Native peoples as a source of red dye.

Golden Corydalis
Corydalis aurea WILLD.
FUMITORY FAMILY

This plant of open woods, roadsides, disturbed places, and streambanks is an erect or spreading branched, leafy biennial or annual. The yellow flowers are irregularly shaped, rather like the flowers of the pea family, with keels at the tips.

The genus name, *Corydalis*, is from the Greek *korydallis*, meaning "crested lark," a reference to the spur of the petal resembling the spur of a lark. The species name, *aurea*, means "golden." Corydalis are generally considered poisonous because they contain isoquinoline and other alkaloids. Some poisoning of livestock has been reported.

Black Twinberry (Bracted Honeysuckle)

Lonicera involucrata (RICH.) BANKS EX SPRENG.

HONEYSUCKLE FAMILY

This plant is a shrub that grows up to two metres tall in moist woods and along streambanks. The flowers are yellow and occur in pairs from the axils of the leaves. The flowers are overlain by a purple to reddish leafy bract. As the fruit ripens, the bracts remain and darken in colour and enlarge. The ripe fruits occur in pairs and are black.

The genus name, *Lonicera*, honours the German botanist Adam Lonitzer. The species name, *involucrata*, refers to the prominent bracts. Some Native peoples believed that the black twinberries were poisonous and would make one crazy. They are bitter to the taste, but serve as food for a variety of birds and small mammals.

Twining Honeysuckle

Lonicera dioica L. VAR. GLAUCESCENS (RYDB.) BUTTERS.

HONEYSUCKLE FAMILY

A flowering vine of the Rocky Mountains, this plant clambers over low bushes and shrubs and around tree trunks at low elevations. The trumpet-shaped flowers cluster inside a shallow cup formed by two leaves that are joined at their bases. The cupped leaves are very distinctive. When the flowers first open they are yellow, turning orange to brick colour with age. The five petals are united into a funnel-shaped tube that has a swollen knob near the base where nectar is accumulated. Insects puncture the knob to obtain the sweet nectar. The flowers are very sweet-scented. The fruits are small red berries, appearing in clusters.

The genus name, *Lonicera*, honours a 16th-century German botanist and physician, Adam Lonitzer. The common name, Honeysuckle, describes the sweet-tasting nectar of the flower. The stems of the Honeysuckles were woven into mats, bags, and blankets by various Native tribes.

Glacier Lily
Erythronium grandiflorum PURSH

LILY FAMILY

This gorgeous lily is one of the first blooms in the spring, often appearing at the edges of receding snowbanks on mountain slopes, thus the common name. The flowers are solitary, bright yellow, and nodding, with the sepals tapered to the tip and reflexed. The leaves, usually two, are attached near the base of the stem and are broadly oblong.

Erythronium is from the Greek *erythros*, meaning "red," referring to the red or pink flowers of some species. The species name, *grandiflorum*, means "large-flowered." Also known locally as Avalanche Lily and Dogtooth Violet, Glacier Lilies are a favoured food of bears. Bears have been observed digging the yellow flowers and bulbs, then leaving them to wilt on the ground, returning days later to eat them. Evidently the bears are aware that the bulbs have an increased sweetness after being exposed to the air. Some Native peoples gathered the bulbs as a food source. The bulbs are inedible when raw, but prolonged steaming converts the indigestible carbohydrates into edible fructose. Drying the bulbs also helps in this process. Glacier Lilies often appear in large numbers, turning the hillsides yellow with their profusion.

Yellowbell

Fritillaria pudica (PURSH) SPRENG.

LILY FAMILY

This diminutive flower is a harbinger of spring, blooming often just after snowmelt in dry grasslands and dry open Ponderosa Pine forests. It can easily be overlooked because of its small size, usually standing only about 15 cm tall. The yellow, drooping, bell-shaped flowers are very distinctive. The flowers turn orange to brick-red with age. The linear to lance-shaped leaves usually number two or three, more or less in a whorl about halfway up the stem. The Yellowbell sometimes appears with two flowers on a stem, but single blooms are more common.

The genus name *Fritillaria* comes from the Latin *fritillus*, "a dice box," most probably a reference to the fruit, which appears as an erect, cylindrical capsule. The species name *pudica* means "bashful" and is probably a reference to the nodding attitude of the flower on the stem. Native peoples gathered the bulbs and used them as a food source, eating them both raw and cooked.

Douglas Maple (Rocky Mountain Maple)
Acer glabrum TORR.

MAPLE FAMILY

This deciduous shrub or small tree is found in moist, sheltered sites from foothills to montane zones. The plant has graceful, wide, spreading branches. The young twigs are smooth and cherry red, turning grey with age. The leaves are opposite and typical of maples—three-lobed with an unequal and sharp-toothed margin. The yellowish-green flowers are short-lived and fragrant, with five petals and five sepals, hanging in loose clusters. The fruits are v-shaped pairs of winged seeds, joined at the point of attachment to the shrub. The fruit is known as a samara.

Acer is Latin for "maple." The species name, *glabrum*, means "smooth, without hair." Native peoples had a variety of uses for this plant, including the manufacture of cordage, cradle frames, teepee pegs and joiners, bows, snowshoes, drum hoops, and fish traps.

Prairie Rocket
Erysimum asperum (NUTT.) DC.
MUSTARD FAMILY

Prairie Rocket grows in dry, sandy grasslands. This erect, robust plant can reach heights approaching a metre. The bright yellow flowers grow at the terminal ends of stout, branching stems and appear in rounded clusters. The stem leaves on the plant are simple, alternate, and lance-shaped.

The genus name, *Erysimum*, is from the Greek *erysio*, meaning "to draw out," a reference to the acrid juices of such plants being used in poultices. The species name, *asperum*, means "rough," a likely reference to the stiff hairs found on the plant. At one time children were treated for worms with a concoction made up of the crushed seeds of this plant mixed in water.

Flixweed
Descurainia sophia (L.) WEBB
MUSTARD FAMILY

Flixweed is a species introduced from Europe and is an invasive weed of waste places, roadsides, and open fields. It can infest areas with tremendous populations. The plant grows up to a metre in height. The stem is thin, occasionally branched, and grey-green in colour. The whole plant is covered in fine hairs. The flowers are very small and pale yellow, clustered at the ends of the stem branches.

The genus name, *Descurainia*, honours Francois Descourain, a French apothecary and botanist of the 18th-century. The genus name, *sophia*, means "wisdom" or "skill," and refers to the wise use made of this plant to treat the disease flix—an old name for dysentery.

Soopolallie (Canadian Buffaloberry)
Shepherdia canadensis (L.) NUTT.

OLEASTER FAMILY

This deciduous shrub grows up to three metres tall and is often the dominant understory cover in Lodgepole Pine forests. All parts of the plant are covered with rust-coloured, shiny scales, giving the whole plant an orange, rusty appearance. The leaves are leathery and thick, green and glossy on the upper surface, while the lower surface is covered with white hairs and sprinkled with rusty-coloured dots. The plant is dioecious, that is, the male and female flowers appear on separate plants. The small, inconspicuous yellow flowers often appear on the branches of the plant prior to the arrival of the leaves. The male flowers have four stamens, while the female flowers have none. In the fall, the female shrubs will be covered with small, translucent berries that are predominantly red.

The genus name, *Shepherdia*, is to honour the 18th-century English botanist John Shepherd. The common name, Soopolallie, is from the Chinook tribe —*soop* meaning "soap" and *olallie* meaning "berry"—a reference to the fact that when beaten in water the red berries produce a pink, soapy froth that some Native peoples liked to drink. The foam is derived from the bitter chemical saponins contained in the berries. Bears seem to relish the berries, and early settlers reported that buffalo browsed them, thus two of the common names. Common names for the plant include Soapberry, Russet Buffaloberry and Bearberry.

Wolf Willow (Silverberry)
Elaeagnus commutata BERNH.

OLEASTER FAMILY

This deciduous shrub grows up to four metres tall and often occurs in dense stands. The twigs are densely covered with rusty brown scales, and the leaves are alternate, oval, silvery in colour, and covered with small scales. The flowers are funnel-shaped and have four yellow lobes, occurring at the leaf axils. The flowers are very fragrant with a distinctive aroma. The fruits are silvery, round to egg-shaped berries and usually persist throughout the winter.

The genus name, *Elaeagnus,* is from the Greek *elaia*, meaning "olive," and *agnos*, meaning "willow." Native people used the tough, fibrous bark of the plant to make bags, baskets, and rope. The berries of the plant were often used as beads for personal adornment. A very similar plant, Russian Olive (*E. angustifolia*), was introduced from Europe and used as a windbreak, but it is a larger plant and has thorns.

Pale Coralroot
Corallorhiza trifida CHATELAIN
ORCHID FAMILY

A plant of moist woods and bogs, this orchid grows to heights of about 15 cm from extensive, coral-like rhizomes. The yellow or greenish-yellow flowers are spread out along the thick stalk, in a cluster at the top of the stem. The flowers often have pale red dots on the lip.

The genus name, *Corallorhiza*, is from the Greek *korallion*, meaning "coral," and *rhiza*, meaning "root," a reference to the coral-shaped rhizomes from which the plant grows. The species name, *trifida*, refers to the three-lobed lip on the flower. All Coralroots are saprophytes, i.e. a plant that absorbs its nutrition from decaying organic matter and lacks any green pigment (chlorophyll) used by most plants for food production. Two other Coralroots occur in the same habitat—the Striped Coralroot (*C. striata*) and the Spotted Coralroot (*C. maculata*). It is interesting to note that the Orchid family is one of the largest plant families in the world, with over 400 genera and more than 20,000 species, most occurring in tropical regions.

Yellow Lady's Slipper
Cypripedium calceolus L.
ORCHID FAMILY

An orchid of bogs, damp woods, and streambanks. The leaves are alternate, with two to four per stem, broadly elliptic, and clasping. The yellow flowers usually occur one per stem and resemble a small shoe. The sepals and lateral petals are similar, greenish-yellow to brownish with twisted, wavy margins. The lower petal forms a prominent, pouch-shaped, yellow lip with purple dotting around the puckered opening.

The genus name, *Cypripedium*, is derived from *Cypris*, another name for Aphrodite, and *pedilon*, which means "foot." The species name, *calceolus*, means "a small shoe." Yellow Lady's Slipper was originally known as *Calceolus mariae*, which translates into "St. Mary's little shoe." Bees enter the opening of the slipper and cannot exit without being covered in pollen. This lovely flower has suffered large-range reductions as a result of picking and attempted transplantation, which almost always fail. There are four species of *Cypripedium* that occur in Alberta and the Rocky Mountains—Seamless Lady's Slipper (*C. acaule*), which has a pink-lipped flower and leafless stem and is quite rare; Mountain Lady's Slipper (*C. montanum*), which is similar to Yellow Lady's Slipper but has a white lip and is somewhat rare; and Sparrow's Egg Lady's Slipper (*C. passerinum*), which has a white or pink lip, shorter, more rounded sepals and petals, and purple spots on the bottom of the lip petal that resemble the spots on a sparrow's egg.

Buffalo Bean (Golden Bean)
Thermopsis rhombifolia NUTT. EX RICHARDS.

PEA FAMILY

A plant of grassy hillsides, roadsides, ditches, and prairies, this member of the pea family can form large clumps from its creeping rootstock. The flower is bright yellow and blooms in crowded clusters atop the stem, which grows to 35 cm. The flower has the typical pea shape, with the keel enclosing the stamens. The leaves are opposite, alternate, compound, and clasping leaflets.

The genus name comes from the Greek *thermos*, meaning "lupine," and *opsis*, meaning "resemblance," because the flowers are similar in shape to those of Lupines. The species name, *rhombifolia*, means "with rhombic (diamond-shaped) leaves." The plant takes its common name from Blackfoot parlance. The Blackfoot believed that when this flower bloomed, it was time to go hunting buffalo, the buffalo having had a chance to fatten on spring grasses. It was not eaten by buffalo because the plant contains poisonous alkaloids. Mountain Goldenpea (*T. montana*) is a similar species that appears in wet meadows at higher elevations. That species can grow up to a metre in height.

Field Locoweed

Oxytropis campestris (L.) DC.

PEA FAMILY

This early-blooming plant is widespread and common in rocky outcrops, roadsides, and dry open woods in the region. The leaves are mainly basal, with elliptical leaflets and dense hairs. The pale yellow, pea-like flowers bloom in clusters at the top of a leafless, hairy stem.

The genus name, *Oxytropis*, comes from the Greek *oxys*, meaning "sharp" or "bitter," and *tropis*, meaning "keel," a reference to the sharp keel on the flower. The species name, *campestris*, means "field loving." The plant is poisonous to cattle, sheep, and horses, owing to its high content of alkaloids that cause blind staggers. This loss of muscle control in animals that have ingested the plant is the origin of the common name for the flower—*loco* being Spanish for "mad" or "foolish."

Yellow Hedysarum
Hedysarum sulphurescens RYDB.

PEA FAMILY

A plant of streambanks, grasslands, open forests, and clearings. The flowers are pea-like, yellowish to nearly white, and drooping, and appear usually along one side of the stem in elongated clusters (racemes). The fruits of the plant are long, flattened, pendulous pods, with conspicuous winged edges and constrictions between each of the seeds.

The genus name, *Hedysarum*, is derived from the Greek *hedys*, meaning "sweet," and *aroma*, meaning "smell." Yellow Hedysarum is also called Yellow Sweet Vetch. It is an extremely important food source for grizzly bears, which eat the roots in the spring and fall.

Yellow Sweet-Clover

Melilotus officinalis (L.) LAM.

PEA FAMILY

A plant of roadsides, ditches, embankments, and pastures, this introduced plant is quite common. It grows to over two metres in height with smooth, leafy, branched stems. The leaflets are slightly toothed and appear in threes. The flowers are yellow and appear in long, narrow, tapered clusters at the top of the plant and in the leaf axils. Each individual flower has a typical pea shape, with standard, wings and a keel. In this flower the standard and wings are about the same length, and the wings are attached to the keel.

The genus name, *Melilotus*, is from the Greek *meli*, meaning "honey," and *lotos*, the name of a clover-like plant in the Mediterranean. *Officinalis* means "yellow." This plant, and a similar plant, White Sweet-Clover (*M. alba*), were introduced as a forage plant for livestock. Both plants contain coumarin, which imparts an overwhelmingly sweet fragrance when you are near the plants or when they are cut for hay.

Antelope Brush (Pursh's Bitterbrush)
Purshia tridentata (PURCH) DC.

ROSE FAMILY

This deciduous shrub grows on dry sites in the plains and foothills of the area and reaches heights of up to two metres. The plant is rigidly branched, and the branches are covered with dense woolly hairs. The flowers are numerous, funnel-shaped, and bright yellow, appearing from the branches of the shrub usually in the spring.

Antelope Bush is important browse for deer and elk, and the seeds from the plant are favourites of small, burrowing mammals such as chipmunks, ground squirrels, and mice. The plants resemble sagebrush, but actually are a member of the Rose family. The plant was first described by Federick Pursh from a specimen collected in Montana by Captain Meriwether Lewis of the Lewis and Clark expedition. Pursh originally named the plant *Tigarea tridentalis*, but later botanists created a new genus and named it in honour of Pursh. The plant is also known by the common names Bitterbrush and Pursh's Bitterbrush.

Early Cinquefoil

Potentilla concinna L.

ROSE FAMILY

A short, spreading perennial that supports two to five flowers per plant. The flowers are bright yellow, with five rounded petals, appearing as solitary flowers atop a leafless stem. The plant is usually less than 10 cm tall overall.

The Early Cinquefoil appears early in the spring and grows low to the ground, often in dry, sandy soil. It is a member of the Rose family, a family that also includes such fruits as apples, plums, cherries, pears, and strawberries. The crushed leaves of most members of the family produce an aroma of bitter almonds.

Shrubby Cinquefoil

Potentilla fruticosa L. (ALSO *Pentaphylloides fruticosa*)

ROSE FAMILY

This low, deciduous shrub is found in dry meadows, on rocky slopes, and in gravelly river courses at mid to subalpine elevations. The leaves are alternate, divided into three to seven (usually five) leaflets that are lightly hairy and greyish-green, and often have curled edges. The flowers are golden yellow and saucer-shaped, with five rounded petals, usually blooming as a solitary at the end of branches. The flowers are often smaller and paler at lower elevations; larger and brighter at higher elevations.

The genus name, *Potentilla*, is from the Latin, *potens*, meaning "powerful," most probably a reference to the supposed medicinal properties of the genus. The species name, *fruticosa*, means "shrubby," and refers to the plant forming a low, rounded bush, usually about a metre high. The common name is from the Latin, *quinque*, meaning "five," and *folium*, meaning "leaf," a reference to the fact that many *Potentilla* species have five leaflets and the flower parts are in fives. Shrubby Cinquefoil is a popular garden ornamental, and is easily propagated from cuttings.

Sticky Cinquefoil
Potentilla glandulosa LINDL.

ROSE FAMILY

This plant inhabits open forests and meadows in low to mid elevations. It grows to about 40 cm tall from a branched rootstock, and the leaves and stems are covered with glandular hairs that exude a sticky, aromatic fluid. The leaves are mainly basal and pinnately divided into five to nine sharply toothed oval leaflets. The flowers are typical of the *Potentillas* and are pale yellow to creamy white, occurring in small, open clusters at the top of the stems.

The species name, *glandulos*a, is a reference to the glandular hairs that cover the plant. This plant, like other members of the family, has a high tannin content and is used as an astringent and anti-inflammatory.

Yellow Avens
Geum aleppicum JACQ.

ROSE FAMILY

An erect, hairy, tall perennial that grows in moist woods, along rivers and streams, and in thickets. The flowers are bright yellow and saucer-shaped with five petals. The flowers usually appear at the tip of a tall, slender stem. The basal leaves of the plant occur in a cluster and are compound and toothed. The top leaflet is heart- to kidney-shaped and deeply lobed.

The genus name, *Geum*, is from the Greek *geyo*, meaning "to stimulate," as the shredded roots of a Mediterranean species were used. A similar species, Large-Leaved Avens (*G. macrophyllum*), occurs in similar habitat, but the terminal leaf is rounded, shallowly lobed, and much larger than the lateral leaves below it on the stem.

Yellow Mountain Avens

Dryas drummondii RICHARDS.

ROSE FAMILY

A plant of gravelly streams and riverbanks, slopes, and roadsides in the foothills and mountains. The yellow flower is solitary and nodding, with black, glandular hairs, blooming on the top of a hairy, leafless stalk. Leaves are alternate, leathery, and wrinkly, dark green above and whitish-hairy beneath. The leaves are rounded at the tip, but wedge-shaped at the base. The margins are scalloped and slightly rolled under. The fruit consists of many achenes, each with a silky, golden-yellow, feathery plume that becomes twisted around the others into a tight spiral and later opens into a fluffy mass, dispersing the seeds on the wind.

The genus name, *Dryas*, was named for the Dryades, daughters of Zeus, the wood nymphs in Greek mythology. The species name, *drummondii*, honours Thomas Drummond, a Scottish naturalist who accompanied Sir John Franklin on his expedition to find the Northwest Passage. Some Native peoples used the plant for medicinal purposes, it being thought that it had healing properties for heart, kidney, and bladder trouble. This small flower likes calcium-rich soil, gravelly streams, and riverbanks, often creating large colonies of flowers. Another *Dryas*, White Mountain Avens (*D. octopetala*), is abundant in the alpine zone and has eight-petalled, white flowers with yellow stamens.

Common St. John's Wort
Hypericum perforatum L.

ST. JOHN'S WORT FAMILY

An introduced noxious weed that grows in disturbed places from valleys to montane forests. The leaves are opposite, longer than wide, and tend to taper toward the base. The leaves have tiny glandular dots, appearing to be pinpricks. The flowers are bright yellow and clustered on the ends of stems. The numerous stamens are distinctive.

This plant is named after St. John the Baptist. The spots on the leaves were said to ooze blood on the day of his execution. Common St. John's Wort is poisonous to livestock and difficult to eradicate once it gets a foothold.

Round-Leaved Violet

Viola orbiculata GEYER

VIOLET FAMILY

This diminutive flower is an early bloomer, appearing right behind the melting snows in moist coniferous forests. The leaves lie flat on the ground and are oval to nearly circular, often remaining green through the winter. The flowers are lemon-yellow and have purplish pencil marking on the lower three petals. The markings direct insects to the source of the nectar.

The species name *orbiculata* is a reference to the shape of the leaves. Candied flowers of this plant are often used for decorating cakes and pastries.

Yellow Wood Violet
Viola glabella NUTT.

VIOLET FAMILY

This beautiful yellow violet occurs in moist woods and often is found in extensive patches. The flowers tend to be a slightly larger size than Round-Leaved Violets (*V. orbiculata*) and have somewhat shorter spurs.

The species name, *glabella*, is from "glabrous," meaning "smooth-skinned," a reference to the smooth leaves. The flower is also commonly referred to as "Smooth Violet" and "Stream Violet."

Red, Orange, and Pink Flowers

This section contains flowers that are red, orange, or pink when encountered in the field. Flowers that are pinkish often can have tones running to lavender, so if you do not find the flower you are looking for, check the Blue/Purple section.

Falsebox

Pachistima myrsinites (PURCH) RAF.

BITTERSWEET FAMILY

This dense evergreen shrub grows low to the ground or up to 60 cm tall in low to mid elevations in coniferous forests. The branches on the plant are reddish-brown and exhibit four ridges. The leaves are opposite, glossy, leathery, and sharply toothed. The relatively inconspicuous flowers are tiny, brick red to maroon in colour, cruciform-shaped with four petals, occurring in clusters along the branches in the leaf axils. The flowers are also quite fragrant.

The genus name, *Pachistima* (also spelled *Paxistima*), is from the Greek *pachus*, meaning "thick," and *stigma*, a reference to the thick stigmas of the flowers on the plant. The species name, *myrsinites*, is from the Greek word for myrrh, the gum resin used in perfumes, medicine, and incense. This reference is undoubtedly to the fragrance of the flowers. The common name of the plant is from the Latin *buxus*, a box being a receptacle that was made from the Boxwood tree, a tree that is reminiscent in form and foliage to this plant. The plant is also known as Mountain Boxwood, Oregon Boxwood, and Mountain-Lover. The branches from the plant are used extensively in the florist trade, even to the point of depleting the native stocks in places.

Red Columbine

Aquilegia formosa FISCH.

BUTTERCUP FAMILY

These beautiful flowers are found in meadows in dry to moist montane to subalpine forests and are among the showiest of all mountain wildflowers. The leaves of the plant are mostly basal and compound, with three sets of three leaflets each. The flowers occur on stems above the basal leaves, and the stem leaves are smaller than the basal leaves and appear with only three leaflets each. The five petals have red spurs above and yellow blades below. The five sepals are red. Numerous stamens extend well beyond the petal blades.

The name Columbine is derived from the Latin *columbina*, meaning "dove like," it being said that the petals resemble a group of doves drinking at a dish. The origin of the genus name, *Aquilegia*, is fraught with some uncertainty. One school of thought attributes the name to the Latin *aquila*, meaning "eagle," a reference to the long, claw-like spur on the flower supposedly resembling an eagle's talon. The other school of thought is that the name comes from *aqua*, meaning "water," and *legere*, meaning "to collect," as little drops of nectar collect at the ends of the spurs. An interesting juxtaposition, with the war symbol eagle on one side, and the peace symbol dove on the other. The species name of the Red Columbine, *formosa*, means "comely" or "beautiful." Bumblebees and butterflies are drawn to the Columbines to collect the nectar. Columbines also appear in western North America in yellow (*A. flavescens*) and blue (*A. brevistyla*).

Western Meadow Rue

Thalictrum occidentale A. GRAY

BUTTERCUP FAMILY

Western Meadow Rue is a dioecious species, which means that the male and female flowers are found on separate plants. The leaves on the plant are very similar in appearance to those of Columbines (*Aquilegia* ssp.), occurring in threes, but this plant's leaves are three times ternate—3 X 3 X 3—for a total of 27 leaflets per leaf. Neither gender of flowers has any petals. The male flower resembles a small wind chime, with the stamens hanging down like tassels. The female flowers resemble small, star-shaped pinwheels. The plant prefers cool, moist forest environments.

The genus name is from the Greek *thallo*, which means "to grow green," probably a reference to the bright green early shoots. The species name, *occidentale*, means "of the west." Native peoples used the plant variously as a medicine, as a love charm, and as a stimulant to horses. In modern times the plant is being investigated for its naturally occurring bioagents in chemotherapy research for cancer.

Wind Flower
Anemone multifida POIR.

BUTTERCUP FAMILY

This plant favours south-facing slopes, grasslands, and open woods.
Like all Anemones, Wind Flowers possess no petals, only sepals.
The flowers are a variety of colours, from white to yellowish to red,
and appear atop a woolly stem. Beneath the flowers are bract-like
leaves attached directly to the stem. The leaves are palmate, with deeply
incised, silky-haired leaflets, somewhat reminiscent of poppy leaves.
The fruits are achenes in a rounded head, which later form a large,
cottony mass.

The common name, Wind Flower, comes from the method of
distributing the long-plumed seeds of the plant. This flower is
also commonly referred to as Cut-Leaved Anemone.

Orange Hawkweed
Hieracium aurantiacum L.

COMPOSITE FAMILY

A plant common to open woods, meadows, roadsides, ditches, and disturbed areas. The orange flower heads appear in a cluster on ascending stalks. The flowers are composed entirely of ray florets, no disk florets. The leaves are in a basal rosette, broadly lanced to spoon-shaped.

The genus name *Hieracium* is from the Greek *hierax*, meaning "hawk," as it was once believed that eating these plants improved a hawk's vision. The species name, *aurantiacum*, means "orange colour." The leaves, stems, and roots produce a milky latex that was used as a chewing gum by British Columbia tribes. A yellow form of Hawkweed (*H. gracile*) also appears in the same habitat as this plant.

Pink Pussytoes (Rosy Pussytoes)
Antennaria microphylla RYDB.

COMPOSITE FAMILY

This mat-forming species is a low perennial that spreads by trailing stems and occurs from valley floors to the subalpine zone. The leaves are spatula-shaped, grey, and hairy on both surfaces. The basal leaves are larger than those on the slender stem of the plant. The flower heads are composite, composed entirely of disk florets, and pinkish in colour. The flower heads are surrounded by several thin, translucent, overlapping bracts.

The soft, fuzzy flower heads of this genus give it the common name— Pussytoes—and a number of species occur in the same general habitat. The species name, *microphylla,* refers to the bracts on the flowers, which are smaller in this species than in other species of *Antennaria.* In the *Antennaria* genus, the male and female flowers are on separate plants.

Spotted Knapweed
Centaurea maculosa LAM.

COMPOSITE FAMILY

This introduced noxious weed inhabits roadsides, ditches, and disturbed areas, and has become a problem in many locales. The plant is many-branched and grows up to over a metre tall from creeping rhizomes. The flowers are heads at the ends of branches, with dark pink or purple disk florets only.

The name Knapweed comes from the ancient English *knap*, meaning "knob" or "bump," a reference to the bumps on the branches of the plant. The genus name, *Centaurea*, is from the Greek *kentaur*, the mythical beast believed to have healing powers. The species name, *maculosa*, means "spotted," a reference to the spots on the bracts of the flowers. It is believed that this plant was inadvertently introduced into North America when its seeds contaminated a shipment of forage crop seeds.

Black Gooseberry (Swamp Currant)
Ribes lacustre (PERS.) POIR.

CURRANT FAMILY

An erect deciduous shrub, growing up to one and a half metres tall, which occurs in moist woods and open areas in the foothills. The branches of the plant have small prickles and stout thorns at leaf and branch bases. The leaves are alternate and shaped like maple leaves, with three to five deeply cut palmate lobes. The flowers are reddish and saucer-shaped, and hang in elongated clusters. The fruits are dark purple to black berries, which bristle with tiny hairs.

The genus name, *Ribes*, is from the Arabic *ribas*, the Moorish medical name for an unrelated rhubarb-like plant that grows in North Africa and Spain. The species name, *lacustre*, is from the Latin *lacus*, meaning "lake," or *lacustris*, meaning "inhabiting lakes." The genus includes all of the Currants and Gooseberries. This plant is also known as Bristly Black Currant. Commonly, members of the *Ribes* genus are divided into Currants and Gooseberries depending upon whether or not the berries are bristly hairy—Currants are not bristly hairy and Gooseberries are. The spines on the plant can cause allergic reactions in some people.

Spreading Dogbane
Apocynum androsaemifolium L.

DOGBANE FAMILY

A fairly common shrub in thickets and wooded areas, the plant has freely branching, slender stems. The leaves are opposite and egg-shaped, and have sharp, pointed tips. The leaves generally droop during the heat of the day. The small, bell-shaped, pink flowers droop from the ends of the leafy stems, usually in clusters. The petal lobes are spreading and bent back, usually with dark pink veins.

The genus name, *Aposcynum*, is from the Greek *apo*, meaning "against" and *kyon*, meaning "dogs," thus the common name. The pods of the plant are poisonous, and it may have been that the pods were used to concoct a poison for dispensing with unwanted dogs. The tough fibers from the stems of Dogbanes were rolled into a strong, fine thread by Native peoples. Several strands plaited together were used for bow strings, and the cord was also used to make fishing nets. When broken, the leaves and stems exude a milky sap. The plant contains a chemical related to digitalis and was once used as a digitalis substitute, but harmful side effects brought an end to that practice. A similar species, Indian-Hemp Dogbane (*A. cannabinum*), occurs in similar habitat, but it is a generally larger species with small flowers and ascending leaves. The two species can overlap and interbreed, producing an intermediate species known as Western Dogbane (*A. medium*).

Fireweed
Epilobium angustifolium L.

EVENING PRIMROSE FAMILY

A plant of disturbed areas, roadsides, clearings, and shaded woods.
This plant is often one of the first plants to appear after a fire. The pink,
four-petalled flowers bloom in long, terminal clusters. Bracts between petals
are narrow. The flowers bloom from the bottom of the cluster first, then
upward on the stem. The leaves are alternate and appear whorled.

The genus name, *Epilobium*, is derived from the Greek *epi*, meaning "upon,"
and *lobos*, meaning "a pod," which refers to the position of the flowers on
top of the seed pod. The species name, *angustifolium*, means "narrow-leafed."
The common name originates from the plant's tendency to spring up from
seeds and rhizomes on burned-over lands. The leaves resemble willow leaves,
hence the alternate name Willow Herb. The young leaves can be used in
salads, and a weak tea can be brewed from the plant. The inner pith can be
used to thicken soups and stews. Fireweed is the floral emblem of Yukon
Territory.

River Beauty
Epilobium latifolium L.

EVENING PRIMROSE FAMILY

Also known as Mountain Fireweed and Dwarf Fireweed, this plant grows as a pioneer, often in dense colonies, on gravelly floodplains and river bars, where the dense leaves and waving pink to purple flowers often obscure the stony ground underneath. River Beauty strongly resembles common Fireweed in appearance, but it has much shorter stems, broader leaves, and larger, more brilliantly coloured flowers. The large and showy, pink to rose purple, four-petalled flowers bloom in a loose, short, leafy inflorescence. The leaves are bluish-green and waxy, with rounded tips.

The genus name, *Epilobium*, is derived from the Greek *epi*, meaning "upon," and *lobos*, meaning "a pod." The species name, *latifolium*, means "broad-leafed." The young leaves can be used in salads, and a weak tea can be brewed from the plant. The inner pith can be used to thicken soups and stews. The plant is also cooling and astringent, and was used by some Native peoples to promote healing of wounds.

Scarlet Butterflyweed
Gaura coccinea PURSH

EVENING PRIMROSE FAMILY

This is a plant of grasslands and dry, south-facing slopes. The flowers are whitish when they first bloom, becoming scarlet or pink as the flower ages. Usually only a few of the flowers on an individual plant bloom at once, and the flowers open fully only at night.

The genus name, *Gaura*, comes from the Greek *gauros*, meaning "superb" or "proud," most probably a reference to the erect nature of the flowers. The species name, *coccinea*, means "scarlet," a reference to the colour of the flower. The common name arises most probably because the flowers are said to be shaped like butterflies.

Elephant's Head
Pedicularis groenlandica RETZ.

FIGWORT FAMILY

A plant of wet meadows, streambanks, and wetland margins. The flowers appear in dense clusters atop a substantial stalk that can reach 50 cm in height. Each of the flowers is reddish-purple to pinkish and has an uncanny resemblance to an elephant's head, with curved trunk and flared ears.

The genus name, *Pedicularis*, is Latin for "louse," and plants of this genus are generally referred to as Louseworts. There was apparently a belief at one time that cattle that ate this plant were more likely to be affected by lice. The species name, *groenlandica*, means "Greenland," though the learned references all seem to be in accord that the first specimens of the plant were found in Labrador, and nobody seems able to explain how Greenland got into the picture. All members of the genus are somewhat parasitic on the roots of other plants, so transplantation is doomed to failure. When encountered, a close examination of this delightful flower is recommended, but be careful of the fragile habitat in which it lives.

Paintbrush

Castilleja miniata DOUGL. EX HOOK.

FIGWORT FAMILY

A plant of alpine meadows, well-drained slopes, open subalpine forests, moist streambanks, and open foothills woods. Paintbrush is widely distributed and extremely variable in colour—from pink to red to yellow to white. The leaves are narrow and sharp-pointed, linear to lance-shaped, usually without teeth or divisions, but sometimes upper leaves have three shallow lobes. The showy red, leafy bracts, which are actually modified leaves, resemble a brush dipped in paint, hence the common name.

The genus name, *Castilleja*, commemorates Domingo Castillejo, an 18th-century Spanish botanist. The species name, *miniata*, refers to the scarlet-red colour minium, an oxide of lead. Although beautiful, this plant should not be transplanted, as it is partially parasitic and does not survive transplanting well.

Various colour phases of *Castilleja*

Thin-Leaved Owl's Clover

Orthocarpus tenuifolius (PURSH) BENTH.

FIGWORT FAMILY

Owl's Clovers are very similar to the Paintbrushes (*Castillejas*),
but the latter are mostly perennial, while the Owl's Clovers are annuals.
In addition, the Paintbrushes have an upper floral lip that is much
longer than the lower lip. In the Owl's Clovers, the upper floral lip
is only slightly, if at all, longer than the lower lip.

The first botanical specimen of Thin-Leaved Owl's Clover was collected
in 1806 by Meriwether Lewis on the banks of what was then called the
Clark's River (now known as the Bitterroot River) while camped at a place
called Travellers' Rest. The Lewis and Clark expedition rested there after
the exhausting crossing of the Bitterroot Mountains. The genus name,
Orthocarpus, is from the Greek *orthos*, meaning "straight," and *karpos*,
which means "fruit," a reference to the seed capsule of the plant.

Strawberry Blite

Chenopodium capitatum (L.) ASCH.

GOOSEFOOT FAMILY

This plant is found from valley to subalpine elevations and is distinctive for its large, triangular or arrowhead-shaped leaves and its dense, fleshy clusters of bright red flowers. The flower clusters appear at the ends of branches on the plant, usually in interrupted bunches, and in the leaf axils.

The genus name, *Chenopodium*, is Greek for "goose foot," a reference to the leaf's resemblance to the foot of a goose. The leaves are rich in vitamins and minerals and are said to resemble spinach when eaten. The flowers are also edible, though most authorities warn against over-indulging in consuming the plant. Some Native peoples used the red flowers as a source for dye, it being bright red initially, then darkening to purple as it ages. Another common name for the plant is Indian Paint.

False Azalea (Fool's Huckleberry)
Menziesia ferruginea SMITH.

HEATH FAMILY

This deciduous shrub is erect and spreading and grows to heights of two metres in moist wooded sites, foothills to montane zones. The twigs of the shrub have fine, rust-coloured sticky glandular hairs and give off a skunky odour when crushed. The leaves are alternate, elliptic and broader above the middle. They are glandular hairy and have a prominent midvein protruding at the tip. The flowers are small, pinkish to greenish-orange, urn-shaped and nodding on long, slender stalks, occurring in clusters at the base of new growth. The fruit is a dark purplish capsule.

The genus name, *Menziesia*, honours Archibald Menzies, a physician and botanist who accompanied Captain George Vancouver in his northwest explorations in the late 18th-century. The species name, *ferruginea*, is Latin meaning "iron rust," a reference to the rusty glands that cover the branches and the leaves. In the fall the leaves of the shrub take on very attractive orange and crimson colours. The common name "False Azalea" arises because the leaves of this plant resemble those of garden Azaleas. Another common name for the plant is "Fool's Huckleberry" because the flowers might be mistaken for those of Huckleberries.

Grouseberry
Vaccinium scoparium LEIBERG.

HEATH FAMILY

This low, deciduous shrub grows up to 20 cm tall and often forms dense ground cover on slopes in the foothills to subalpine zone. The branches are numerous, slender, and erect. The leaves are alternate, ovate, widest in the middle, and sharp-pointed with finely serrated margins. The flowers are small, pinkish, urn-shaped, and nodding, hanging down singly from the leaf axils. The fruits are tiny, edible, bright red berries.

The Grouseberry is a member of the same genus as Blueberries, Huckleberries, and Cranberries. The species name, *scoparium*, is from the Latin *scopula*, meaning "broom-twig," a reference to the close, twiggy stems on the plant. The berries are very small, and some Native peoples gathered them using combs. Small mammals and birds eat the berries. Grouse eat all parts of the shrub, thus the common name "Grouseberry."

Huckleberry

Vaccinium membranaceum DOUGL.

HEATH FAMILY

This erect, densely branched, deciduous shrub grows to heights of one and a half metres at mid to high elevations in dry to moist coniferous forests. The leaves are lance-shaped to elliptic with pointed tips and finely toothed margins. The leaves turn red or purple in the fall. The flowers are creamy pink and urn-shaped, nodding on slender stalks. The fruits are black to dark purple berries 8–10 mm across.

Without question, the berry of this plant is among the most sought-after wild berries that occur in the Rocky Mountains—by human consumers, birds, and bears. The sweet taste of the berry is distinctive, and the berries are used to make jams, syrups, and liqueurs. Among those who harvest the berries, picking sites are jealously guarded. My son once asked a picker where he found the berries. The picker answered: "Sonny, I would sooner tell you that I was sleeping with your wife than I would where I pick huckleberries!"

Kinnikinnick (Bearberry)

Arctostaphylos uva-ursi (L.) SPRENG.

HEATH FAMILY

This trailing or matted evergreen shrub grows low to the ground and has long branches with reddish, flaky bark and leathery, shiny, green leaves. The flowers are pale pink and urn-shaped, appearing in clumps at the ends of the stems. The fruits are dull red berries.

The genus name, *Arctostaphylos*, is from the Greek *arktos*, meaning "bear," and *staphyle*, meaning "bunch of grapes." The species name, *uva-ursi*, is Latin for "bear's grape." The berries are apparently relished by bears and birds, though they tend to be dry and mealy to humans. They are edible and have been used as food, prepared in a variety of ways. The berries remain on the plant through the winter. One of the common names, Kinnikinnick, is believed to be of Algonquin origin and means "something to smoke," a reference to the fact that some Native peoples used the leaves of the plant as a tobacco.

Pine-Drops

Pterospora andromedea NUTT.

HEATH FAMILY

This purple or reddish-brown saprophyte (a plant that gets its nutrients from decaying plant or animal matter) stands up to a metre tall or more, and lives in deep humus of coniferous or mixed woods. The plants grow singly or in clusters, but they are rare. The leaves are mostly basal and resemble scales. The stem stands erect and is covered with glandular hairs. The flowers are cream-coloured to yellowish and occur in a raceme that covers roughly the top half of the stalk. The petals are united into an urn shape and hang downward off bent flower stalks, like small lanterns. The stalks of the plant will remain erect for a year or more after the plant dies.

The genus name, *Pterospora*, is from the Greek *pteron*, meaning "wing," and *sporos*, meaning "seed," a reference to the winged appearance of the seeds. The species name, *andromedea*, refers to Andromeda of Greek mythology. To review the story of Andromeda, see Western Mountain Heather. I am at a complete loss as to how the taxonomist connected this plant to that particular myth, and I have so far been unable to explain the connection.

Pink Wintergreen
Pyrola asarifolia MICHX.

HEATH FAMILY

An erect perennial that inhabits moist to dry coniferous and mixed forests and riverine environments. The flowers are shaped like an inverted cup or bell, nodding, waxy, pale pink to purplish-red, and have a long, curved projecting style. The leaves are basal in a rosette. The leaves have a leathery appearance and are shiny, rounded, and dark green.

The genus name, *Pyrola*, is derived from Latin *pyrus*, which means "a pear," probably a reference to the leaves being pear-shaped. The species name, *asarifolia*, is from the Latin *asarum*, meaning "ginger," and *folium*, meaning "leaf," a reference to the similarity between the leaves of this plant and those of wild ginger. Wintergreen leaves contain acids that are effective in treating skin irritations. Mashed leaves of *Pyrola* species have traditionally been used by herbalists in skin salves and poultices for snake and insect bites. They are called wintergreen, not because of the taste, but because the leaves remain green during the winter. Like orchids, many of these plants require a specific fungus in the soil to grow successfully, and transplantation should not be attempted. Two other species of *Pyrola*, Greenish Flowered Wintergreen (*P. chlorantha*) and One-Sided Wintergreen (*P. secunda*), occur in similar habitat.

Prince's-Pine (Pipsissewa)

Chimaphila umbellata (L.) BART. SSP. *occidentalis* (RYDB.) HULT.

HEATH FAMILY

This small evergreen shrub grows to heights of 30 cm in coniferous woods. The dark green, glossy leaves are narrowly spoon-shaped and saw-toothed, and occur in whorls. The flowers are pink, waxy, saucer-shaped, and nodding on an erect stem above the leaves. The fruits of the plant are dry, round, brown capsules that often overwinter on the stem.

The genus name, *Chimaphila*, comes from the Greek *cheima*, meaning "winter," and *philos*, meaning "loving," descriptive of the evergreen leaves. Prince's-Pine is also known as "Pipsissewa," an adaptation of the Cree name for the plant—*pipisisikweu*—meaning "it breaks into small pieces," a reference to a substance in the leaves that was said to dissolve kidney and gall stones. The plant was often used to make a medicinal tea. Both Native peoples and settlers to North America used the plant for a variety of medicinal purposes.

Western Bog-Laurel (Swamp Laurel)
Kalmia microphyllia (HOOK.) HELLER

HEATH FAMILY

This low-growing evergreen shrub occurs in cool bogs and on streambanks and lakeshores in the subalpine and alpine zones. The leaves are leathery, dark green above and grayish-white beneath, often with the margins rolled under. The flowers are pink to rose-coloured with the petals fused together to form a saucer or bowl, appearing on a reddish stalk. There are ten purple-tipped stamens protruding from the petals.

The genus name, *Kalmia*, is to honour Peter Kalm, a student of Carolus Linnaeus at Uppsala University in Sweden. Linnaeus was a prominent botanist who developed binomial nomenclature for plants. The leaves and flowers of this plant contain poisonous alkaloids that can be fatal to humans and livestock if ingested.

Twinflower
Linnaea borealis L.

HONEYSUCKLE FAMILY

This small, trailing evergreen, a member of the honeysuckle family, is common in coniferous forests, but easily overlooked by the casual observer. This plant sends runners creeping over the forest floor, over mosses, fallen logs, and stumps. At frequent intervals the runners give rise to the distinctive Y-shaped stems, 5–10 cm tall. Each fork of the stem supports at its end a slightly flared, pink to white, trumpet-like flower that hangs down like a small lantern on a tiny lamppost. The flowers have a sweet perfume that is most evident near evening.

The genus name, *Linnaea*, honours Carolus Linnaeus, the Swedish botanist who is the father of modern plant nomenclature. It is said that this flower was his favourite among the thousands of plants he knew. The species name, *borealis*, means "northern," referring to the circumpolar northern habitat of the plant. Some Native peoples made a tea from the leaves of this plant.

Nodding Onion
Allium cernuum ROTH

LILY FAMILY

All *Allium* species smell strongly of onion and have small flower clusters at the top of the leafless stalk. Nodding Onion is the most common species in the Rocky Mountain region and is easily identified by its pink, drooping or nodding inflorescence.

The stem gives off an onion odour when crushed and is said to be one of the better-tasting wild onions. Native peoples gathered the bulbs and ate them raw and cooked; used them for flavouring other foods; and dried them for later use. Bears and ground squirrels also use this plant in their diets. *Allium* is the Latin name for garlic, from the Celtic *all*, meaning "hot" or "burning," because it irritates the eyes. The species name, *cernuum*, refers to the crook in the stem of the plant just below the flower.

Sagebrush Mariposa Lily
Calochortus macrocarpus DOUGLAS.

LILY FAMILY

This is a large lily of dry grasslands and open Ponderosa forests in the Rocky Mountain trench. This species is similar to the Three Spot Mariposa Lily (*C. apiculatus*), but its pinkish to purplish petals are more pointed and the gland at the base of each petal is crescent shaped—very different from the Three Spot Mariposa Lily. This plant grows in more arid environments and blooms later than does the Three Spot Mariposa Lily.

Mariposa is the Spanish word for "butterfly," and the markings on the flower are said to resemble those on some butterflies, thus the common name. The genus name, *Calochortus*, is from the Greek word *kallos*, meaning "beautiful," and *chortos*, meaning "grass." The species name, *macrocarpus* means "large seed." As with many other lilies, picking the flower of this plant will kill the plant because picking the flower deprives the bulb of needed nourishment. The range of this plant has been severely restricted over the years by grazing cattle. The plant will not accept transplantation, so it is best to enjoy it in the wild where it grows.

Tiger Lily
Lilium columbianum HANSON.

LILY FAMILY

True lilies are recognized by their large, showy flowers; smooth, unbranched stems; and whorls of narrow, lance-shaped leaves. Tiger Lilies can have up to 30 flowers per stem. The orange to orange-yellow flowers are downward-hanging, with curled-back petals, with deep red to purplish spots near the centre. The flowers are very similar to Western Wood Lilies (*L. philadelphicum*), but the Wood Lily petals form more of a chalice shape, without the petals curling back like those of the Tiger Lily.

The common name for the Tiger Lily most probably comes from the spotting on the petals. There was once a superstition that smelling the Tiger Lily would give you freckles. The bulbs of Tiger Lilies were used as food by Native tribes and were said to have a peppery taste. Like other lilies, this one will die if the flower is picked. The bulb depends upon the flower for nutrients, and if the flower is removed, the bulb will starve and die.

Western Wood Lily

Lilium philadelphicum L. (ALSO *Lilium umbellatum* PURSH)

LILY FAMILY

Considered by many to be among the most beautiful wildflowers of the
Rocky Mountains, the Western Wood Lily grows in moist meadows, dense
to open woods, and edges of aspen groves. The leaves are numerous, lance-
shaped, smooth, and alternate on the stem, except for the upper leaves,
which are in whorls. Each plant may produce from one to five bright orange
to orange-red flowers, each with three petals and three similar sepals. The
petals and the sepals are orange at the tip, becoming yellowish and black
or purple-dotted at the bases. The anthers are dark purple in colour.

Lilium is the Latin name for the plant. There are several stories as to how the
species name originates. One explanation holds that Linnaeus received his
specimens of the plant from a student in Philadelphia. Another explanation
holds that the name comes from the Greek words *philos*, meaning "love," and
delphicus for the ancient wooded oracle at Delphi, hence "wood lover." The
Western Wood Lily is the floral emblem of Saskatchewan, but it is becoming
increasingly rare, owing to picking of the flower. The bulb from which the
flower grows depends upon the flower for nutrients, and will die if the flower
is picked. The plants do not survive transplantation well, but can be grown
from seeds, though the propagated plants might not flower for several years.
The bulbs were eaten by some Native tribes, but were generally considered
to be bitter. The Blackfoot treated spider bites with a wet dressing of the
crushed flowers. Western Wood Lilies are often confused with Tiger Lilies
(*L. columbianum*), which are coloured similarly, but the petals on the Tiger
Lily are curled backwards, while the petals on the Wood Lily are held in a
chalice shape.

90

Wild Bergamot
Monarda fistulosa L.

MINT FAMILY

This showy flower inhabits grasslands and open woods, blooming in the summer months. The stems of the plant are erect and square, with a strong and distinctive odour of mint. The stem is topped by a dense cluster of pink to violet flowers. The leaves are opposite, triangular to ovate in shape, and pointed at the ends.

Native peoples used Bergamot medicinally for various ailments, from acne to bronchial complaints to stomach pains. Some tribes used the plant as a perfume, meat preservative, and insect repellant. It is also reported that the plant was used ceremonially in the Sun Dance. The genus name, *Monarda*, honours an early Spanish physician, Nicholas Monarddez, who described many North American plants. The species name, *fistulosa*, means "tubular," a reference to the flower shape. Local common names include Horsemint, Bee Balm, and Oswego Tea.

Spotted Coralroot
Corallorhiza maculata RAF.

ORCHID FAMILY

A plant of moist woods and bogs, this orchid grows from extensive coral-like rhizomes. The purple to brownish flowers have purple or red spots on the white lip. A number of flowers appear on each stem, loosely arranged up the stem. The leaves are reduced to sheaths that surround and somewhat conceal the base of the purplish stem.

The genus name, *Corallorhiza*, is from the Greek *korallion*, meaning "coral," and *rhiza*, meaning "root," a reference to the rhizomes from which the plant grows. Two other Coralroots occur in the same habitat as the Spotted—the Pale Coralroot (*C. trifida*) and the Striped Coralroot (*C. striata*). The Coralroots are saprophytes, i.e. plants that absorb their nutrition from decaying organic matter and lack any green pigment (chlorophyll) used by most plants for food production.

Striped Coralroot

Corallorhiza striata LINDL.

ORCHID FAMILY

A plant of moist woods and bogs, this orchid grows from extensive coral-like rhizomes. The pink to yellowish-pink flowers have purplish stripes on the sepals, and the lowest petal forms a tongue-shaped lip. A number of flowers appear on each stem, loosely arranged up the stem. The leaves are reduced to sheaths that surround and somewhat conceal the base of the purplish stem.

The genus name, *Corallorhiza*, is from the Greek *korallion*, meaning "coral," and *rhiza*, meaning "root," a reference to the rhizomes from which the plant grows. Two other Coralroots occur in the same habitat as the Striped—the Pale Coralroot (*C.trifida*) and the Spotted Coralroot (*C. maculata*). Of the three, the Striped Coralroots have the largest flowers. The Coralroots are saprophytes, i.e. plants that absorb their nutrition from decaying organic matter and lack any green pigment (chlorophyll) used by most plants for food production.

Venus' Slipper
Calypso bulbosa (L.) OAKES

ORCHID FAMILY

An orchid found in shaded, moist, coniferous forests. The flowers are solitary and nodding on leafless stems. The flower has pinkish to purplish sepals and mauve side petals. The lip is whitish or purplish, with red to purple spots or stripes, and is hairy yellow inside. The flower is on the top of a single stalk with a deeply wrinkled appearance. A small but extraordinarily beautiful flower that blooms in the early spring, often occurring in colonies.

The Venus' Slipper has many common names, including Fairy Slipper and Calypso Orchid. The genus name, *Calypso*, is derived from Greek mythology, Calypso being the daughter of Atlas. *Calypso* means "concealment" and is very apt, given that this flower is very easy to miss, being small, delicate, and growing in out-of-the-way places. The species name, *bulbosa*, refers to the bulb-like corm from which the flower grows. Do not attempt to transplant this flower. It needs specific fungi in the soil to grow successfully.

Red Clover
Trifolium pratense L.

PEA FAMILY

A European species now well-established in North America, Red Clover grows to heights of 60 cm in low to mid elevations. The leaves occur in threes, often displaying a white, crescent-shaped spot near the base. The flowers are pea-like, pinkish to purple, and up to 200 of them occur in a dense head 2–3 cm in diameter at stem tops, with two leaves immediately below the flower head.

All clovers have leaves in threes and flowers in dense heads. The name Clover is from the Latin *clava*, meaning "club," and more particularly the triple-headed cudgel carried by Hercules. That club bears a resemblance to the shape of the leaf on Clover. The suit of clubs in cards comes from the same root and has the same shape. White Clover (*T. repens*) is a similar plant in the same habitat. White Clover has a creeping stem and white to pinkish flowers on longer stalks. Herbalists favour Red Clover in the treatment of skin problems.

Bitterroot
Lewisia rediviva PURSH

PURSLANE FAMILY

A plant of dry grasslands and sagebrush slopes, the Bitterroot was first catalogued by Captain Meriwether Lewis of the Lewis and Clark expedition, and the genus is named for him. The strikingly beautiful flowers are deep pink to sometimes white, and have about 15 narrow petals. The flowers occur on such short stalks that they virtually appear to rest on the soil's surface. The flowers open only in the sun. The leaves are all basal, appearing in the spring, but withering and receding into the ground prior to the flower blooming.

The Bitterroot was used as a food source and a trading item by many Plains Indian tribes, and, indeed, wars were fought over Bitterroot collection grounds. The roots were dug in the early spring, then peeled and cooked or dried for winter use. The members of the Lewis and Clark expedition found the roots very bitter to the taste, hence the common name. Lewis first collected the root in Montana in 1806. His pressed, dried specimen was shipped east for examination, and when examined many months after collection it still showed signs of life. When planted, it promptly grew, giving it its species name, *rediviva*, meaning "restored to life." The Bitterroot River in Montana takes its name from the plant (having originally been named Clark's River), and the plant is the floral emblem of Montana.

Old Man's Whiskers (Three Flowered Avens)
Geum triflorum PURSH

ROSE FAMILY

This plant is widespread on dry plateaus at low to subalpine elevations, open grasslands, and arid basins. The flowers bloom in early spring and are dull purplish to pinkish, hairy, and nodding at the top of the stem. The flowers usually occur in a cluster of three, though some plants will have as many as five flowers on a single stem. The flowers remain semi-closed and do not open out flat. They were once described to me as "looking like three very tired ballerinas at the close of a performance."

Three Flowered Avens are also known as Old Man's Whiskers and Prairie Smoke. Old Man's Whiskers is probably a reference to the appearance of the fruits—achenes with feathery styles that resemble grey whiskers. These fruits are distributed by winds, and it is said that they sometimes occurred in such abundance on the unbroken prairies that when the seeds blew it looked like smoke over the prairies, hence the common name Prairie Smoke. Some Native peoples boiled the roots to make a tea and use as a medicine for colds, flu, and fever.

Prickly Rose
Rosa acicularis LINDL.

ROSE FAMILY

The floral emblem of Alberta, the Prickly Rose is a deciduous shrub with freely branched stems and thorns at the base of each leaf. The flowers are pink with five broad petals. Leaves are oblong and notched, somewhat hairy below. The Prickly Rose will easily hybridize with other members of the rose family and can be difficult to specifically identify. The fruits are dark red, round to oval, fleshy hips with sepals remaining on top like a beard. They are high in vitamin C content and can be a favourite food of many species of birds. The hips can be used to make a delicious jelly.

The foliage and young stems of wild roses are browsed by wild ungulates and domestic livestock. Native peoples used the plants for medicinal purposes and used the thorns for fishing lures. Wild Roses produce root suckers and can be very invasive and aggressive in spreading.

White, Green, and Brown Flowers

This section includes flowers that are predominantly white or cream-coloured, green, or brown when encountered in the field. Given that some flowers fade to other colours as they age, if you do not find the flower you are looking for in this section, check the other sections in the book.

Sitka Alder

Alnus crispa PURSH

BIRCH FAMILY

This deciduous shrub grows up to five metres tall and is commonly found from low elevations to timberline in forests, clearings, and seepage areas. The leaves are broadly oval with rounded bases, pointed tips, and double-toothed margins. The male and female flowers develop with the leaves. The male catkins are long and drooping; the female catkins are short and cone-like.

Native peoples made various uses of Sitka Alder, from basket making to smoking fish and meat to making a reddish dye. Alders improve soil fertility by fixing nitrogen in nodules on their roots

Buckbrush Ceanothus (Snowbrush)

Ceanothus velutinus DOUGL. EX HOOK.

BUCKTHORN FAMILY

This erect evergreen shrub grows to heights of up to two metres on well-drained slopes in the montane and subalpine forests, and is abundant after a forest fire. The aromatic leaves are alternate and oval, finely toothed, dark green on the top, and greyish underneath. A varnish-like, sticky substance covers the upper leaf surface, giving it a shiny appearance and a strong aroma. The leaves have three prominent veins that radiate from the leaf base. The flowers bloom in the early summer and are tiny, white, and heavily scented, and occur in dense clusters on reddish stalks at the ends of the branches.

The common name, Buckbrush, comes from the fact that deer and elk often browse on this plant in the winter. The leaves and stems of the plant contain a toxic glucoside—saponin—but ungulates seem to have no ill effects from eating the plant. The seeds of the plant can survive in the soil for up to two centuries, and fire stimulates them to germinate. Young shrubs grow rapidly after a fire, but are eventually shaded out by trees.

Baneberry

Actaea rubra (AIT.) WILLD.

BUTTERCUP FAMILY

A plant of moist, shady woods and thickets, often found along streams. Baneberry is a tall, often branching, thick-stemmed, leafy perennial. The flower is a dense, white, cone-shaped cluster that appears on top of a spike. The fruit is a large, shiny cluster of either red or white berries. At the time of flowering there is no way to determine whether the berries of a particular plant will be red or white.

The common name of the plant comes from the Anglo Saxon word *bana*, meaning "murderer" or "destroyer"—undoubtedly a reference to the fact that the leaves, roots, and berries of this plant are extremely poisonous. As few as two berries can induce vomiting, bloody diarrhea, and finally cardiac arrest or respiratory paralysis. The genus name *Actaea* comes from the Greek *aktaia*, meaning "elder tree," as the leaves are similar to elder leaves. The species name *rubra* is Latin for "red," a reference to the berries. There have been reports of children who have died as a result of eating the berries.

Canada Anemone
Anemone canadensis L.

BUTTERCUP FAMILY

A plant of moist grasslands and woods, aspen groves, and riverine thickets. The leaves are toothed and deeply divided into three to five lobes on long leaf stalks. The leaves are light green with fine hairs above and below. They are long veined and attached to the stem in a whorl. The flowers are composed of five white, petal-like sepals that are rounded at the tip, with soft hairs underneath.

The genus name is said to come from the Greek word *anemos*, which means "wind"—most probably a reference to the fact that the wind distributes the long-stemmed fruits of the plant. The whole plant is poisonous and can cause skin irritation if handled, and severe gastroenteritis and ulceration if ingested.

Northern Anemone
Anemone parviflora MICHX.

BUTTERCUP FAMILY

Also known as Few Flowered Anemone, this plant prefers moist soils and streamside habitats in the subalpine and alpine areas. The stalk stands up to 30 cm and supports a single flower with five or six creamy-white, hairy sepals. On the stem below the flower there is a ring of three deeply cleft leaves.

The genus name, *Anemone*, is most probably derived from the Greek, *anemo*, meaning "wind," a reference to the fact that the seeds of members of the genus are distributed by the wind. These flowers are also referred to as Wood Anemones.

Cow Parsnip

Heracleum lanatum MICHX.

CARROT FAMILY

A plant of shaded riverine habitat, streambanks, and moist, open aspen woods, this plant can attain heights of over two metres. The flowers are distinctive in large, compound, umbrella-shaped clusters (umbels) composed of numerous white flowers with white petals in fives. The leaves are compound in threes, usually very large, softly hairy, deeply lobed, and toothed.

Heracleum refers to Hercules, likely because of the plant's large size. Cow Parsnip is also locally known as Indian Celery and Indian Rhubarb. The roots were cooked and eaten by some Native peoples, though there are some sources that say they are poisonous. The Blackfoot roasted the young spring stalks and ate them. They also used the stalks in their Sun Dance ceremony. Caution should be taken to distinguish this plant from the violently poisonous Water Hemlock (*Cicuta maculata*).

Large-Fruited Desert-Parsley

Lomatium macrocarpum (NUTT.) COULT. AND ROSE.

CARROT FAMILY

A low growing perennial herb common in dry climates, open slopes, and gravelly areas. The leaves on this plant are fern-like in appearance and hairy. The flowers are white to purplish in colour and occur in large, umbrella-shaped clusters at the top of the multiple stems.

Native peoples used the plant for food, usually digging up the taproots before the plant bloomed in the spring. The roots are said to have a peppery taste and were eaten raw or cooked. Two common names for the plant are Indian Carrot and Indian Sweet Potato.

Sharptooth Angelica (Lyall's Angelica)
Angelica arguta NUTT.

CARROT FAMILY

A plant of shaded riverine habitat, streambanks, and moist, open woods, this plant can attain heights of over two metres. The numerous white flowers are arranged in compound umbels. The leaves are twice compound, with large leaflets that are sharply toothed, as is reflected in the common name for the plant. The lateral leaf veins are directed to the ends of the teeth on the leaf margin, unlike Water Hemlock (*Cicuta maculata*), which has similar flowers but the leaf veins are directed to the notch between the teeth on the leaf margin.

The genus name, *Angelica*, is from the Latin *angelus*, meaning "an angel." There appear to be several schools of thought as to how this reference to angels arose. One school of thought has it that a revelation was made by an angel to Matthaeus Sylvaticus, a 14th-century physician who compiled a dictionary of medical recipes, of the beneficial medicinal properties of the plant. Another school of thought is that the flower usually blooms near to the time of the celebration of the feast of St. Michael the Archangel. The species name, *arguta*, is Latin, meaning "sharp-toothed." The other common name, Lyall's Angelica, is in honour of David Lyall, a British botanist and geologist who collected specimens while working on the boundary survey between Canada and the United States in the 1880s. Angelicas are highly prized by herbalists for treating digestive disorders.

Water Hemlock
Cicuta maculata L. (ALSO *Cicuta douglasii*)

CARROT FAMILY

A plant of marshes, river and stream banks, and low, wet areas. The plant produces several large, umbrella-like clusters (compound umbels) of white flowers appearing at the top of a sturdy stalk. The leaves are alternate, with many bipinnate and tripinnate leaflets that are lance-shaped. The side veins in the leaflets end between the notched teeth on the leaflets, rather than at their points.

The genus name, *Cicuta*, is the Latin name of some poisonous member of the carrot family. While lovely to look at, with its umbrella-shaped clusters of flowers on sturdy stems, the Water Hemlock is considered to be perhaps the most poisonous plant in North America. All parts of the plant are poisonous as testified to by several common names which include Children's Bane, Beaver Poison, and Death of Man. The toxin, cucutoxin, acts on the central nervous system and causes violent convulsions, followed by paralysis and respiratory failure. Some Native peoples used the powdered root as a poison on arrows. If you touch this plant, or cut it with an implement for any reason, wash your hands and the implement immediately and thoroughly. A similar plant appears in the same habitat—the Sharptooth Angelica (*Angelica arguta*)—but the leaf veins in Angelica run to the points of the teeth margins on the leaves.

Common Cattail
Typha latifolia L

CATTAIL FAMILY

This plant is very common and well-recognized from slough and pond margins and along streams in the area. The leaves are long, flat, and strap-like, and the unisexual flowers are cylindrical, dense flower masses. The top of the mass consists of the pollen-bearing male flowers, while the bottom includes the tightly packed pistillate flowers.

Cattails were used extensively by Native peoples. The leaves of the plants were woven into mats, hats, bags, and even capes; the seed heads were used as an absorbent in diapers, as well as for stuffing in mattresses and pillows; the young flowers and rhizomes were eaten. Cattails are also very important cover and food source for a variety of birds and small mammals. Captain William Clark of the Lewis and Clark expedition noted in his journal that members of the expedition had purchased hats and mats made from the plant from Natives near the mouth of the Columbia River in late 1805.

Broad-Leaved Pussytoes (Broad-Leaved Everlasting)
Antennaria neglecta GREENE
COMPOSITE FAMILY

This plant is common to prairie and open woods habitats. The white to cream-coloured flowers have disk florets only and occur in dense clusters at the top of a slender stem. Male and female flowers grow on separate plants. The leaves are mostly basal.

The common name for these plants is a reference to the fuzzy flower heads resembling feline toes. The genus name, *Antennaria*, is from the Latin *antenna*, which means "feeler," most probably a reference to the pappus hairs on the male flowers, which resemble antennae on insects. The species name, *neglecta*, means "neglected" or "overlooked," probably a reference to the relatively inconspicuous growth.

Ox-Eye Daisy
Leucanthemum vulgare LAM.

COMPOSITE FAMILY

An invasive Eurasian perennial from a well-developed rhizome, this plant frequents low to mid elevations in moist to moderately dry sites such as roadsides, clearings, pastures, and disturbed areas. The flowers are solitary composite heads at the end of branches, with white ray flowers and yellow disk flowers. The basal leaves are broadly lance-shaped or narrowly spoon-shaped. The stem leaves are oblong and smaller.

Daisy is from the Anglo-Saxon *day's eye*, a reference to the fact that the English daisy closes at night and opens at sun-up. One of the most common and recognizable wildflowers in North America, the Ox-Eye Daisy is very prolific and will overgrow large areas if not kept in check. A similar flower, Scentless Chamomile (*Matricaria perforata*) occurs in similar habitat and is often confused with Ox-Eye Daisy. To confirm the identity, closely inspect the leaves on the plant in issue. Scentless Chamomile has much thinner leaflets, and they are much more dissected than are those of Ox-Eye Daisy.

Pearly Everlasting
Anaphalis margaritacea (L.) BENTH. AND HOOK.

COMPOSITE FAMILY

This plant grows in gravelly, open woods and subalpine meadows in the Rocky Mountains. There are numerous stem leaves, alternately attached directly to the stem. The leaves are lance-shaped and light green, with very soft, fuzzy hairs. The white flowers occur in a dense, rounded terminal cluster. The male and female flowers occur on separate plants. The flowers have only disk florets and no ray florets, and often have a brown spot at the base.

The common name, Pearly Everlasting, comes from the fact that the dried flowers often last for a long time. The species name, *margaritacea*, means "of pearls," and is undoubtedly a reference to the shape of the flowers. The plant resembles Pussytoes, but this plant has more leaves than Pussytoes, and the leaves are not reduced in size from the base to the top of the plant, as they are in most Pussytoes.

Small-Leaved Everlasting
Antennaria parvifolia NUTT.

COMPOSITE FAMILY

This plant is a relative of the Pussytoes and is found in arid slopes and grasslands in southeastern British Columbia, often establishing extensive colonies. The plant is small, reaching only 10–20 cm in height. The leaves are grey in colour and woolly on both sides. The flowers are tightly packed heads, usually appearing in five parts on top of a short stem.

The genus name, *Antennaria*, is from the Latin *antenna*, meaning "a feeler," thought to come from the fact that the pappus hairs of the male flowers have swollen tips and are said to resemble the antennae of butterflies. Members of the genus were often chewed by Native peoples and also used in tobacco mixtures.

Tufted Fleabane
Erigeron caespitosus NUTT.

COMPOSITE FAMILY

A plant of dry, open places, south-facing slopes, coulees, and eroded badlands, this small, white, daisy-like flower can grow in large bunches or clusters. The ray florets are usually white, but sometimes bluish or pink. The numerous, narrow petals surround central yellow disk florets. The basal leaves are grey-green, short and hairy, and lance- or spoon-shaped.

The common name, Fleabane, originates from an ancient belief that bundles of related species would discourage fleas. The genus name, *Erigeron*, is from the Greek, *eri*, meaning "spring," and *geron*, meaning "old man" and probably is a reference to the over-all hairiness of the species. The species name, *caespitosus*, means "tufted," and probably refers to the growth habit. Tufted Fleabane contains a volatile, turpentine-like oil, and the liquid from the boiled roots and leaves was used to treat various aliments, such as rheumatism, hemorrhoids, and gonorrhea.

Fleabanes are difficult to tell apart, and are often difficult to tell from Asters. Fleabanes generally have narrower, more numerous ray florets than Asters. In addition, if you check the involucral bract—the small green cup under the flower—and see that all of the bracts are the same length, then you have a Fleabane. If some of the bracts are obviously shorter, you have an Aster.

White Hawkweed

Hieracium albiflorum L.

COMPOSITE FAMILY

A plant common to moist to dry, open woods, meadows, and clearings at low to mid elevations. The white flower heads appear in an open inflorescence on ascending stalks. The flowers are composed entirely of ray florets with no disk florets. The leaves are broadly lance-shaped and often have wavy-toothed edges with bristly hairs on the upper surfaces.

The genus name *Hieracium* is from the Greek *hierax*, meaning "hawk," as it was once believed that eating these plants improved a hawk's vision. The species name, *albiflorum*, means "white-flowered." The leaves, stems, and roots of all members of the genus produce a milky latex when broken. Two similar species, Orange Hawkweed (*H. aurantiacum*) and Slender Hawkweed (*H. gracile*) occur in similar habitat.

Yarrow

Achillea millefolium L.

COMPOSITE FAMILY

A plant of dry to moist grasslands, open riverine forests, aspen woods, and disturbed areas. The individual white flower heads appear in a dense, flat-topped or rounded terminal cluster. The ray florets are white to cream-coloured (sometimes pink), and the central disk florets are straw-coloured. The leaves are woolly, greyish to blue-green and finely divided, almost appearing to be a fern. Yarrow can occur in large colonies.

The common name is derived from the name of a Scottish parish. The genus name, *Achillea,* is in honour of Achilles, the Greek warrior with the vulnerable heel, who was said to have made an ointment from this plant to heal the wounds of his soldiers during the siege of Troy. The species name, *millefolium,* means "thousand leaves," in reference to the many finely divided leaf segments. Yarrow contains an alkaloid called achillean that reduces the clotting time of blood. It appears a number of Native peoples were aware of this characteristic of the plant and made a mash of the crushed leaves to wrap around wounds.

Northern Black Currant (Skunk Currant)
Ribes hudsonianum RICHARDS

CURRANT FAMILY

An erect, deciduous shrub, growing up to two metres tall at low to mid elevations in moist to wet forests. This plant does not have thorns, but does have yellow resin glands dotting its smooth bark. The leaves are alternate, maple-leaf-shaped with three to five rounded lobes. The flowers are white and saucer-shaped, and occur in spreading to erect clusters. The flowers have a strong smell that some people find objectionable. The fruits are black, speckled with resin dots, and said to have a particularly bitter taste.

Berries of all currants are high in pectin and can make excellent jams and jellies, though the raw berries are often insipid.

Sticky Currant
Ribes viscosissimum PURSH

CURRANT FAMILY

This plant is a shrub that grows up to two metres high in damp woods and openings. It does not have the prickles of many gooseberries and currants. The flowers are bell-shaped, yellowish-white, and often tinged in pink. The flowers and leaves are covered in glandular hairs that are sticky to the touch. The fruits are blue-black, sticky, and not considered edible.

The species name, *viscosissimum*, is derived from the Latin *viscosus*, meaning "sticky" or "viscid." The first known botanical specimen was collected by Meriwether Lewis in Idaho in 1806. Lewis's note on the plant says that the fruit is "indifferent & gummy."

Bunchberry (Dwarf Dogwood)
Cornus canadensis L.

DOGWOOD FAMILY

A plant of moist, coniferous woods, often found on rotting logs and stumps. The flowers are clusters of inconspicuous greenish-white flowers set among four white, petal-like, showy bracts. The leaves are in a terminal whorl of four to seven, all prominently veined. The leaves are dark green above, lighter underneath. The fruits are bright red berries.

The genus name, *Cornus*, is Latin for "horn" or "antler," possibly a reference to the hard wood of some of this species. Another school of thought is that the inflorescence of the plant bears a resemblance to the cornice piece, a knob on cylinders used for rolling up manuscripts. *Canadensis* is a reference to Canada, this plant being widely distributed across the country in the boreal forests. Bunchberry's common name is probably derived from the fact that the fruits are all bunched together in a terminal cluster. The plant is also known as Dwarf Dogwood. A Nootka legend has it that the Bunchberry arose from the blood of a woman marooned in a cedar tree by her jealous husband. The plant is reported to have an explosive pollination mechanism wherein the petals of the mature but unopened flower buds suddenly reflex and the anthers spring out, casting pollen loads into the air. When an insect brushes against the tiny bristle at the end of one petal it triggers this explosion.

Red Osier Dogwood

Cornus stolonifera L.

DOGWOOD FAMILY

This willow-like shrub that grows up to three metres high, often forms impenetrable thickets along streams and in moist forests. The reddish bark is quite distinctive, and it becomes even redder with the advent of frosts. The leaves are heavily veined, dark green above and pale underneath. The flowers are small and greenish-white, and occur in a flat-topped cluster at the terminal ends of stems. The fruits are small, white berries, appearing in clumps.

The common name, Osier, appears to be from the Old French *osiere*, meaning "that which grows in an osier-bed (streambed)." Native peoples used the branches of the plant to fashion fish traps, poles, and salmon stretchers. This plant is extremely important winter browse for moose.

Eyebright
Euphrasia arctica LANGE

FIGWORT FAMILY

These beautiful plants are tiny, standing only 10–15 cm tall. The white flowers are worth investigating closely, revealing delicate purple markings and yellow hues inside the small flower. The leaves are very distinctive, being opposite and alternate and very prominently toothed. The flowers occur in the axils of the leaves near the top of the stem.

A number of Eyebrights occur in the world, mostly in northern latitudes. The sample shown here was photographed in the Nordic Tracks above the town of Kimberley, British Columbia. At the time the plant was photographed in the summer of 2004, it appeared to be unknown to local botany enthusiasts.

Parrot's Beak
Pedicularis racemosa DOUGL. EX BENTH.

FIGWORT FAMILY

This lovely plant favours upper montane and subalpine environments.
The white flower has a very distinctive shape that deserves close examination
to appreciate its intricacy. The flowers appear along a purplish stem that
grows up to 35 cm tall. The leaves are simple and lance-shaped to linear,
and have distinctive fine, sharp teeth on the margins.

The genus name, *Pedicularis*, is Latin for "louse." There was apparently a
belief at one time that cattle that ate plants of this genus were more likely
to be affected by lice. Parrot's Beak takes its common name from the long,
slender, downward-turned beak on the upper lip of the petals. Another
common name, Sickletop Lousewort, is a reference to the shape of
the flowers.

White Geranium
Geranium richardsonii FISCH. AND TRAUTV.

GERANIUM FAMILY

A plant of moist grasslands, open woods, and thickets, this plant is very similar to Sticky Purple Geranium (*G. viscosissimum*), except it has white to pinkish flowers with purple veins. The petals have long hairs at the base. The leaves are not sticky and are hairy only along the veins of the lower sides of the leaves. The fruits are like those of the Sticky Purple Geranium—that is, capsules with long beaks shaped like a crane's or stork's bill.

The fruit capsules are said to open explosively, with the beak splitting lengthwise from the bottom and catapulting the seeds away from the parent plant. White Geraniums seem to prefer partially shaded growing locations, rich in humus. The species name, *richardsonii*, is in honour of Sir John Richardson, a 19th-century Scottish botanist assigned to Sir John Franklin's expedition to the Arctic in search of the Northwest Passage.

Devil's Club
Oplopanax horridum (J. SMITH) MIQ.

GINSENG FAMILY

If there were a contest for the meanest plant in the woods, this one would almost certainly qualify. The Devil's Club is aptly named. It has club-shaped, woody stems that grow to over two metres in height, and the stems are covered in stiff, sharp spines. The leaves are large, shaped like very large maple leaves, with sharp spines on their veins and leaf stalks, and sharp teeth on their margins. The flowers are small, white globe shapes that are arranged along a central flower stalk up to 25 cm long. The fruits are a mass of shiny, red berries.

The genus name, *Oplopanax*, is from the Greek *hoplon*, meaning "weapon." The species name, *horridum*, comes from the same root as "horrible." The spines of the plant easily break off in skin, and the punctures occasioned will quickly become sore and inflamed. In spite of all this, the plant is quite handsome and regal. It also has a number of medicinal properties and has been used by Native peoples and herbalists to treat such diverse ailments as arthritis, diabetes, cataracts, and indigestion. It is recommended that this plant be given a good inspection, but do not get too close.

Wild Sarsaparilla
Aralia nudicaulis L.

GINSENG FAMILY

This plant prefers the dark woods of the moist montane forests. The leaves are up to 50 cm long, arising singly from an underground stem. Each leaf has a long, bare stalk that terminates in three to five leaflets each. The leaflets are up to 15 cm long and are sharply toothed and pointed at the ends. The flowers arise from a short stem near ground level, well below the spreading leaflets. The flowers are tiny, whitish-green and arranged in three round-shaped umbels.

The genus name, *Aralia*, is the Latinized form for the French *aralie*, the Quebec Habitant name for the plant. The species name, *nudicaulis*, means "bare stem," a reference to the leafless flower stalk. The plant was used as a stimulant in sweat lodges by some Native peoples, and was also used in a variety of other medicinal ways.

Fringed Grass-of-Parnassus

Parnassia fimbriata KOENIG

GRASS-OF-PARNASSUS FAMILY

These plants abound in riverine habitat, pond edges, and boggy places. The white flowers are very delicate-looking in construction. The flowers appear as singles on a slender stem, with five white petals with greenish or yellowish veins. The lower edges of the petals are fringed with hairs. Alternating fertile and sterile stamens are characteristic of this genus. The leaves are mostly basal and broadly kidney-shaped. A single leaf clasps the flowering stem about halfway up.

The name of this plant seems to present some confusion. One school of thought is that the genus name, *Parnassia*, is from Mount Parnassus in Greece, said to be a favourite retreat of the God Apollo. Another school of thought holds that the name comes from a description of the plant written in the first century by Dioscorides, a military physician for the Emperor Nero. When the description was translated, "grass" was included in the translation, and it stuck. There is no doubt that this plant is not even remotely grass-like. A similar species, Northern Grass-of-Parnassus (*P. palustris*) occurs in the same habitat, but it does not have the fringed margins of Fringed Grass-of-Parnassus.

Greenish Flowered Wintergreen
Pyrola chlorantha sw.

HEATH FAMILY

An erect perennial that inhabits moist to dry coniferous and mixed forests and riverine environments. The flowers have five greenish-white, waxy petals and a long style attached to a prominent ovary. The flowers have a bell shape and are distributed on short stalks up the main stem. The leaves are basal in a rosette. The leaves have a leathery appearance and are shiny, rounded, and dark green.

The genus name, *Pyrola*, is derived from Latin *pyrus*, which means "a pear," probably a reference to the leaves being pear-shaped. Wintergreen leaves contain acids that are effective in treating skin irritations. Mashed leaves of *Pyrola* species have traditionally been used by herbalists in skin salves and poultices for snake and insect bites. They are called "wintergreen," not because of the taste, but because the leaves remain green during the winter. Like orchids, these plants require a specific fungus in the soil to grow successfully, and transplantation should not be attempted. Another species of *Pyrola*, Pink Wintergreen (*P. asarifolia*), is similar in shape and occurs in similar habitat, but has pink flowers. White-Veined Wintergreen (*P. picta*), also known as Painted Pyrola, also occurs in similar habitat. It differs from Greenish Flowered Wintergreen in that it has longer, lance-shaped leaves with extraordinarily beautiful white mottling along the veins of the upper surface of the leaves.

Labrador Tea
Ledum groenlandicum (OEDER) HULT.

HEATH FAMILY

This evergreen, much-branched shrub is widespread in low to subalpine elevations in peaty wetlands and moist, coniferous forests. The flowers are white and numerous, with five to ten protruding stamens in umbrella-like clusters at the ends of branches. The leaves are alternate and narrow, with edges rolled under. They are deep green and leathery on top, with dense, rusty hairs underneath.

The leaves, used fresh or dried, can be brewed into an aromatic tea, but should be used in moderation to avoid drowsiness. Excessive doses are reported to act as a strong diuretic. The aromatic leaves were used in barns to drive away mice and in houses to keep away fleas.

One-Sided Wintergreen

Pyrola secunda L. (ALSO *Orthilia secunda* [L.] HOUSE)

HEATH FAMILY

A small forest dweller that grows to 5–15 cm tall. The white to yellowish-green flowers lie on one side of the arching stalk, arranged in a raceme of six to ten flowers, sometimes more. The flowers resemble small street lights strung along a curving pole. The straight style sticks out beyond the petals, with a flat, five-lobed stigma. The leaves are basal, egg-shaped, and finely toothed at the margins.

One-Sided Wintergreen is included in the *Pyrola* genus by some taxonomists, but is put into the *Orthilia* genus by others. *Orthilia* is from the Greek *orthos*, meaning "straight," most probably a reference to the straight style. The species name, *secunda*, comes from the Latin *secundus*, meaning "next" or "following," a reference to the flowers that follow each other on the same side of the stem. Once seen, this delightful little flower is unmistakable in the woods.

Oval-Leaved Blueberry
Vaccinium ovalifolium GREENE
HEATH FAMILY

This deciduous shrub grows to heights of over two metres in low to subalpine elevations in moist to wet, coniferous forests, clearings, and bogs. The pale pink flowers are urn-shaped, and appear singly at the leaf bases. The flowers may precede the arrival of the leaves. The berries are blue-black, dusted with a pale bluish bloom. The berries are somewhat large for wild blueberries and have a pleasant flavour. The leaves are oval, blunt and rounded at the ends, and usually lack teeth on the margins.

The genus *Vaccinium* includes all of the wild Blueberries, Cranberries, and Huckleberries. The species name, *ovalifolium*, refers to the shape of the leaves. Another common name applied to this plant is Blue Huckleberry.

Painted Pyrola (White-Veined Wintergreen)
Pyrola picta SM.

HEATH FAMILY

An erect perennial that inhabits moist coniferous and mixed forests in the extreme southern parts of the area. The flowers are similar to Greenish Flowered Wintergreen (*P. chlorantha*)—bell-shaped, waxy, and distributed along the main stalk—but the leaf of this plant is the distinguishing feature. The leaves of Painted Pyrola are thick, glossy, and green, with extraordinarily beautiful white mottling along the veins of the upper surface. This mottling gives the plant its other common name, "White-Veined Wintergreen." The pale areas on the leaf's surface are caused by a lack of chlorophyll, which indicates the partially parasitic nature of the plant.

The genus name, *Pyrola*, is derived from Latin *pyrus*, that means "a pear," probably a reference to the leaves of some members of the genus being pear shaped. Wintergreen leaves contain acids which are effective in treating skin irritations. Mashed leaves of *Pyrola* species have traditionally been used by herbalists in skin salves and poultices for snake and insect bites. They are called "wintergreen," not because of the taste, but because the leaves remain green during the winter. Like orchids, these plants require a specific fungus in the soil to grow successfully, and transplantation should not be attempted. Another species of *Pyrola*, Pink Wintergreen (*P. asarifolia*), is similar in shape and occurs in similar habitat, but has pink flowers.

Single Delight
Moneses uniflora (L.) A. GRAY (ALSO *Pyrola uniflora*)

HEATH FAMILY

This delightful little forest dweller is also known as One Flowered Wintergreen, and it inhabits damp forests, usually on rotting wood. The plant is quite tiny, standing only 10 cm tall, and the single white flower, open and nodding at the top of the stem, is less than 5 cm in diameter. The flower looks like a small, white umbrella offering shade. The leaves are basal, oval, and evergreen, attached to the base of the stem. The style is prominent and tipped with a five-lobed stigma.

The genus name, *Moneses*, is from the Greek *monos*, meaning "solitary," and *hesia*, meaning "delight," a reference to the delightful single flower. Other common names include Wood Nymph and Shy Maiden. In Greek mythology nymphs were nature goddesses, beautiful maidens living in rivers, woods, and mountains, and once you see this diminutive flower, the common names seem completely appropriate.

Western Mountain Heather

Cassiope mertensiana (BONG) D. DON

HEATH FAMILY

This matting plant occurs in the subalpine and alpine zones. The flowers are white, bell-shaped, and nodding at the end of the stems. The leaves are opposite, evergreen, and pressed so closely to the stems that the stems are all but hidden. The foliage forms low mats on the ground.

The genus name, *Cassiope*, is from Greek mythology. Cassiopeia was the wife of Cepheus, the king of the Ethiopians. She was vain and boastful, claiming that her beauty exceeded that of the sea nymphs. This claim offended and angered the sea nymphs, who prevailed upon Poseidon, the god of the sea, to send a sea monster to punish Cassiopeia by ravaging the land. In order to save the kingdom, the Ethiopians offered Cassiopeia's daughter, Andromeda, as a sacrifice, chaining her to a rock. Perseus, the Greek hero who slew the Gorgon Medusa, intervened at the last minute to free Andromeda and slay the monster. In astronomy, the constellation Perseus stands between Cassiopeia and Andromeda, still defending her today. The species name, *mertensiana*, honours F.C. Mertens, an early German botanist. In fact, Western Mountain Heather is not a heather at all, but a heath.

White Rhododendron
Rhododendron albiflorum HOOK.

HEATH FAMILY

An erect and spreading deciduous shrub that grows up to two metres high and inhabits cool, damp woods, often establishing dense communities under the conifer canopy. The leaves are oblong to lance-shaped and are covered with fine, rusty-coloured hairs. The leaves turn to beautiful shades of crimson and orange in the fall of the year. The flowers are large (up to 3 cm across), white, and cup-shaped, and are borne singly or in small clusters around the stem of the previous year's growth. The petals are joined to each other for about half of their length, and ten stamens are visible inside the flower. The flowers are deciduous and fall off the plant as a whole, often littering the forest floor with what appear to be intact flowers.

The genus name, *Rhododendron*, is from the Greek *rhodon*, meaning "rose," and *dendron*, meaning "tree." The species name, *albiflorum*, means "white-flowered." This plant is often referred to as Mountain Misery because it grows in dense communities, with branches trailing downhill, making it difficult for hikers to move through it. All parts of the plant contain poisonous alkaloids that are toxic to humans and livestock.

Black Elderberry

Sambucus racemosa SSP. *pubens* L. VAR. *melanocarpa* (GRAY)

HONEYSUCKLE FAMILY

This is a tall, deciduous shrub that grows to heights of several metres from low to subalpine elevations along streams, in moist thickets and clearings, and in shady forests. The opposite, branching stems of the plant are woody, stout, and filled with pith in the centre. The leaves are pinnately compound, with five to seven leaflets that are pointed, lance-shaped, and sharply toothed. The flowers are white to creamy and occur in large, pyramid-shaped clusters. The flowers have a relatively strong, unpleasant odour. The fruits are black or purplish-black berries that appear in the late summer.

The fruits of this plant have long been used as a food source. Wine and jellies can be produced from the berries. Bears and birds seem quite partial to the fruits. The branches of the plant have been hollowed out to make whistles, drinking straws, pipe stems, and blowguns, but that practice is discouraged because the branches of the plant contain glycosides and are poisonous. Two other Elderberries occur in the same range—Blue Elderberry (*S. cerulea*), which has waxy, blue fruits, and Red Elderberry (*S. racemosa* var. *arborescens*), which has red fruits.

Blue Elderberry
Sambucus cerulea RAF.

HONEYSUCKLE FAMILY

This is a tall, deciduous shrub that grows to heights of several metres on streambanks and in open forests. The opposite, branching stems of the plant are woody, stout, and filled with pith in the centre. The leaves are pinnately compound, with five to nine leaflets that are up to 15 cm long. The flowers are white to creamy and occur in large, flat-topped clusters at the summit of the branches. The fruits are waxy, pale powdery-blue berries that appear in the late summer.

The fruits of this plant have long been used as a food source. Wine and jellies can be produced from the berries. Bears seem quite partial to the fruits. The branches of the plant have been hollowed out to make whistles, drinking straws, pipe stems, and blowguns, but that practice is discouraged because the branches of the plant contain glycosides and are poisonous.

Snowberry
Symphoricarpos albus (L.) BLAKE

HONEYSUCKLE FAMILY

This common deciduous shrub occurs from coast to coast in North America and is found from prairies to lower subalpine zones in well-drained open or wooded sites. There are several subspecies that are so alike that dissection and magnification are required to tell one from the other. The shrub is erect and can attain heights of two metres. The branches are opposite and slender and, on close examination, covered with tiny hairs. The leaves are opposite, elliptic to oval, and pale green. The flowers are white to pink and broadly funnel-shaped, occurring in clusters at the ends of the twigs. The stamens and style do not protrude from the flower. The fruits are waxy, white, berry-like drupes that occur in clusters and often persist through the winter.

The berries of this plant were not eaten by Native peoples, and many considered them poisonous. In fact, some Natives called the berries Corpse Berries and Ghost Berries. Some Native peoples believed that these white berries were the ghosts of Saskatoon Berries and thus part of the spirit world and not to be tampered with by the living.

Utah Honeysuckle (Red Twinberry)
Lonicera utahensis WATS.

HONEYSUCKLE FAMILY

This erect, deciduous shrub grows up to two metres tall. The leaves are opposite, elliptical to oblong, with smooth edges and blunt tips. The creamy-white flowers are trumpet-shaped and appear in pairs on a single stalk from the leaf axils. The fruits are red berries that are joined at the base.

Some Native peoples ate the berries of Utah Honeysuckle, which were said to be a good emergency source of water because the berries are so juicy. The flowers are frequented by hummingbirds.

Bronzebells
Stenanthium occidentale A. GRAY

LILY FAMILY

This lily of moist woods, streambanks, meadows, and slopes has grass-like leaves that emerge from an onion-like bulb. The bell-shaped flowers are greenish-white, flecked with purple, and have six sharply pointed tips that twist backward, exposing the interior of the blossom. Ten or more graceful and fragrant flowers are hung along the length of the stem, drooping down.

The genus name, *Stenanthium*, is derived from the Greek *steno*, meaning "narrow," and *anthos*, meaning "flower." The appropriateness of this name will be testified to by any photographer who has tried to photograph this species in even a slight breeze. The species name, *occidentale*, means "western." Without question, this flower is extraordinarily attractive in its detail.

Clasping-Leaved Twisted-Stalk
Streptopus amplexifolius (L.) DC.

LILY FAMILY

This member of the lily family grows in moist, shaded forests and has a widely branching, zigzag stem, with numerous sharply pointed, parallel-veined leaves that encircle the stem at each angular bend. The plant varies in height from 30 to 100 cm. The glossy leaves often conceal the small, pale white or greenish flowers that dangle on curving, thread-like stalks from the axil of each of the upper leaves. In fact, one can walk by the plant without noticing the flowers hiding under the leaves. The flowers have strongly reflexed petals and sepals, and appear to be hanging on the plant like small spiders dangling on fine webs. The fruits of the plant are very handsome orangish-red, oval berries.

The genus name, *Streptopus*, is derived from the Greek *streptos*, meaning "twisted," and *pous*, meaning "foot," referring to the twisted flower stalks. The species name, *amplexifolius*, comes from the Latin *amplexor*, meaning "to surround," and *folius*, meaning "a leaf."

Death Camas
Zigadenus venenosus WATS.

LILY FAMILY

This plant of moist grasslands, grassy slopes, and open woods grows from an onion-like bulb that has no oniony smell. The leaves are mainly basal and resemble grass, with prominent mid-veins. The greenish-white, foul smelling-flowers appear in tight clusters atop an erect stem, each flower having three virtually identical petals and sepals. There are yellowish-green, v-shaped glands (nectaries) near the base of the petals and sepals.

The genus name, *Zigadenus*, is derived from the Greek *zygos*, meaning "yoke," and *aden*, meaning "gland," a reference to the shape of the nectary at the base of each petal and sepal. The species name, *venenosus*, is Latin for "very poisonous." Death Camas contains poisonous alkaloids and is probably even more toxic than its close relative, White Camas (*Z. elegans*), which appears in the same general habitat, but blooms later. These plants have been responsible for killing many people and animals. When the flowers are missing, Death Camas and White Camas are difficult to distinguish from Blue Camas (*Camassia quamash*), another lily, the bulb of which was commonly used as a food source by Native peoples and early settlers.

Fairybells

Disporum trachycarpum (S. WATS.) B. AND H.

LILY FAMILY

A plant of shaded poplar woods, streambanks, and riverine environments, this delightful flower blooms in early summer. The flowers are creamy-white and occur in drooping pairs, generally bell-shaped at the end of branches. The leaves of the plant are generally lance-shaped with pointed ends. The fruits are generally red, egg-shaped berries, occurring in pairs.

The genus name, *Disporum*, is from the Greek *dis*, meaning "double," and *spora*, meaning "seeds." The species name, *trachycarpum*, means "rough-fruited." The berries from Fairybells are edible, but said to be bland. They are a favoured food of many rodents and birds.

False Solomon's Seal

Smilacina racemosa (L.) DESF.

LILY FAMILY

A lily of moist woods, rivers and streambanks, thickets, and meadows, that can grow up to half a metre tall. The flowers are small and white, arranged in a branching panicle that is upright at the end of the stem. The leaves are broadly lance-shaped, numerous, and alternate, gradually tapering to a pointed tip, with prominent parallel veining, sometimes folded at the midline. The fruit is a red berry flecked with maroon.

The genus name, *Smilacina*, means "a small Smilax," and refers to this plant's resemblance to plants in the genus *Smilax*. The species name, *racemosa*, indicates that the plant has a raceme arrangement for the flowers. This name is somewhat confusing in that a raceme is an unbranched cluster of flowers on a common stalk. The flower arrangement on this plant is more precisely referred to as a panicle—a branched flower cluster that blooms from the bottom up. A very similar plant lives in the same habitat—the Star Flowered Solomon's Seal (*S. stellata*)—but it has significantly fewer flowers.

Indian Hellebore
Veratrum viride AIT.

LILY FAMILY

A tall, stout, often fuzzy-haired perennial with many leaves that inhabits moist forests, thickets, bogs, wet meadows, and avalanche chutes. The greenish flowers occur in long, open, drooping clusters along a substantial stalk that arises from the centre of the generally basal leaves. The stamens are yellow-tipped. Perhaps the most distinctive feature of this robust plant is the leaves. They are large and dull green, with long, closed sheaths at the base. Each leaf is broadly elliptic with pointed tip and a prominently veined or ribbed smooth surface above and hairy underside. The basal leaves appear well before the flowers and seem to whirl up from the earth, dwarfing all other plants around them.

This plant is also known as Green False Hellebore, a reference apparently to the genus name, *Veratrum*, being used in ancient time to apply to a true hellebore that was a member of the *Helleborus* family. The genus name is from the Latin words *vere*, meaning "true," and *atrum*, meaning "black," a reference to the black roots of the true hellebore. The species name, *veride*, means "green." This plant contains very toxic alkaloids which can cause symptoms very like heart attacks. People have died from eating it and, indeed, the Alberta Blackfoot are said to have used the plant to commit suicide. The plant is most dangerous early in the growing season and is said to have caused accidental poisonings among cattle and sheep. Early American settlers boiled the roots and combed the resulting liquid through their hair to kill lice.

Queen's Cup
Clintonia uniflora (SCHULT.) KUNTH

LILY FAMILY

This beautiful perennial lily grows from slender rhizomes, with the flowers appearing on short and leafless stalks. The flowers are about 5 cm in diameter and are usually solitary, white, and cup-shaped, appearing at the top of an erect, hairy stalk. The plant has two or three leaves that are oblong or elliptical and shiny with hairy edges, and appear at the base of the flowering stalk.

The genus name, *Clintonia*, is named for DeWitt Clinton, a New York state governor and botanist of the 19th century. As the season progresses, the flower is replaced by a single, deep blue, beadlike berry, giving the plant another common name of Beadlily. The bead was used by some Native peoples to make a blue dye.

Star Flowered Solomon's Seal

Smilacina stellata (L.) DESF.

LILY FAMILY

A lily of moist woods, rivers and streambanks, thickets, and meadows. The flowers are white, star-shaped, and arrayed in a loose, short-stalked cluster, often on a zigzag stem. The leaves are broadly lance-shaped, numerous, and alternate, gradually tapering to a pointed tip, with prominent parallel veining, sometimes folded at the midline. The fruit is a cluster of green to cream-coloured berries with maroon to brown stripes.

One theory holds that the common name is a reference to the six-pointed star in the seal of King Solomon. The species name, *stellata*, is Greek for "star-like." Another closely related species is found in the same habitat—False Solomon's Seal (*S. racemosa*). The flowers of False Solomon's Seal are much more numerous and decidedly smaller than those of Star Flowered Solomon's Seal. The flowers of False Solomon's Seal were described by one observer as a "creamy foam of flowers," a rather apt description.

Sticky False Asphodel

Tofieldia glutinosa (MICHX.) PERS.

LILY FAMILY

A lily of wet bogs, meadows, and streambanks, the distinctive feature of this plant is the upper portion of the flowering stem, which is glandular and sticky. The white flowers are clustered atop the stem, with dark anthers conspicuous against the white of the petals. The basal leaves are linear, lance-shaped, and grass-like, and are about half the length of the stem.

The plant resembles the European Asphodel, thus the common name. The genus name, *Tofieldia*, is to honour 18th-century British botanist Thomas Tofield. The species name, *glutinosa*, is a reference to the sticky stem below the flower. Mosquitoes are often trapped on the sticky stem of this plant, which acts as natural flypaper.

Three Spot Mariposa Lily
Calochortus apiculatus BAKER

LILY FAMILY

A plant of open coniferous woods, dry sandy or gravelly slopes, and moist fescue grassland in the montane zone. This perennial lily grows from a bulb as a single-leafed plant, producing one to five flowers from each plant. The flower is white to yellowish-white with three spreading petals, fringed at the margins. Each petal is hairy on the inner surfaces, with a purplish gland at the base. These purple glands give the flower one of its common names— Three-Spot Tulip. Three narrow, white sepals appear between the petals.

"Mariposa" means "butterfly" in Spanish, it being thought that the markings on some Mariposa Lilies resemble the markings on a butterfly's wings. The genus name, *Calochortus*, is from the Greek *kallos*, meaning "beautiful," and *chortos*, meaning "grass." The species name, *apiculatus*, refers to the slender-tipped anthers. Some Native tribes used the bulbs of the plant as food, it being eaten raw, cooked, or dried for later use. The Blackfoot looked upon them as famine food only. Picking the flower will destroy the plant because the bulb depends upon the flower for nutrients. Picking the flowers can significantly reduce the range and distribution of lilies. The plants do not transplant well, and cultivation attempts have consistently failed.

White Camas
Zigadenus elegans PURSH

LILY FAMILY

This plant of moist grasslands, grassy slopes, and open woods grows from an onion-like bulb that has no oniony smell. The greenish-white, foul-smelling flowers appear in open clusters along an erect stem. Yellowish-green, v-shaped glands (nectaries) sit near the base of the petals and sepals. The leaves are mainly basal and resemble grass, with prominent mid-veins.

The genus name, *Zigadenus*, is from the Greek *zygos*, meaning "yoke," and *aden*, meaning "gland," a reference to the shape of the nectary at the base of each petal and sepal. The species name, *elegans*, means "elegant." Though elegant, indeed, these plants are extremely poisonous, containing very toxic alkaloids, particularly in the bulbs. These plants have been responsible for killing many people and animals. When the flowers are missing, White Camas and a closely related species, Death Camas (*Z. venenosus*), are difficult to distinguish from Blue Camas (*Camassia quamash*), another lily, the bulb of which was commonly used as a food source by Native peoples and early settlers. Other common names for White Camas include Mountain Death Camas, Green Lily, and Showy Death Camas.

Yucca
Yucca glauca NUTT.

LILY FAMILY

This large member of the lily family is a coarse, erect plant that can attain great heights on dry, exposed slopes and in sandy and gravelly soil. The cream-coloured, waxy flowers are large, drooping, and bell-shaped, occurring in clumps and clusters at the terminal end of the stiff, upright stem of the plant. The basal leaves are very distinctive. They are stiff, narrow, and long, with extremely sharp, hard tips. The leaves can penetrate clothing, lending to the plant one of its common names, Spanish Bayonet.

Another common name for the plant is Soapweed, a reference to the fact that the plants contain saponin, a glucoside that forms a soapy foam when dissolved in water. Yucca is generally a desert plant, and it only occurs in Alberta in the Milk River region.

Northern Bedstraw
Galium boreale L.

MADDER FAMILY

A plant common to roadsides and woodlands. The flowers are tiny, fragrant, and white, occurring in dense clusters at the top of the stems. The individual flowers are cruciform (cross-shaped), with each having four spreading petals that are joined at the base. There are no sepals. The smooth stems are square in cross-section and bear whorls of four narrow, lance-shaped leaves, each with three veins.

The common name for this plant is a reference to a practice of Native peoples to use the dried, sweet-smelling plants to stuff mattresses. The roots of the plants were a source of red and yellow dyes. The genus name, *Galium*, is from the Greek *gala*, which means "milk," a reference to the fact that country folk used the juice of another similar plant to curdle milk. The species name, *boreale*, means "northern," a reference to the distribution of the plant worldwide.

Morning Glory

Calystegia sepium (L.) R. BR. (ALSO *Convolvulus sepium* L.)

MORNING GLORY FAMILY

Morning Glory is a twining, climbing, or trailing vine that grows from slender, spreading rhizomes. The flowers are 3–6 cm across, white to pinkish in colour, and trumpet- or funnel-shaped. The leaves are alternate and arrowhead-shaped, and the flowers appear solitary in the leaf axils. The flowers usually close when it is dark, overcast, or raining.

The genus name, *Calystegia*, is from the Greek *kalyx*, meaning "cup," and *stegos*, meaning "cover," a reference to the bracts that cover the sepals on the flower. This plant is also commonly called Hedge Bindweed, Lady's Nightcap, and Bell-Bind. A closely related plant, Field Bindweed, is a noxious weed that creeps over crops and covers everything within its reach. Unlike many climbing plants, the Bindweeds cannot support their stems and tendrils, so they wind their stems tightly around available supports. Under favourable conditions, a Bindweed stem will complete an encirclement of a support in under two hours' time.

Reflexed Rock Cress
Arabis holboellii HORNEM.

MUSTARD FAMILY

This plant is widespread in prairie zones, especially on gravelly slopes and in dry, open woods. The plant stands up to 70 cm tall. The basal leaves form a rosette, and the stem leaves are numerous, narrow, lance-shaped, and clasping on the stem. The flowers are white to pinkish, occurring on reflexed stalks, hanging down along the stem and in a terminal cluster.

The genus name, *Arabis*, is said to have originated in Arabia, where numerous Rock Cresses occur. The species name, *holboellii*, honours 19th-century Danish botanist Carl Peter Holboell. Rock Cresses are edible and are said to have a taste similar to radishes. The leaves and flowers are often added to salads and sandwiches. The common name, "cress," is said to be derived from an old Indo-European word that meant "to eat" or "nibble." A similar species, Drummond's Rock Cress, occurs in similar habitat, but is shorter and holds its pods erect or slightly spreading.

Stinging Nettle

Urtica dioica L. SSP. *gracilis* (AIT.) SELANDER

NETTLE FAMILY

This plant occurs in moist mountain forests, thickets, and meadows at various elevations. The plant has a square stem and can grow to heights of up to two metres. The leaves are narrowly lance-shaped, opposite, simple, toothed, and apparently wrinkled. The leaves are shiny on top, up to 15 cm long, tapered to the tip, and covered with small hairs. The flowers are inconspicuous and green, and occur in drooping clusters from the leaf axils. Both male and female flowers appear on the same plant.

The genus name, *Urtica*, comes from the Latin *uro*, meaning "to burn," a very understandable reference to anybody who has had the misfortune of getting involved with the stinging hairs that cover this plant. Interestingly, despite the nasty skin irritation that can result from casual contact, the leaves of the plant are considered important both as a food source and as a medicine. The plant is rendered harmless when cooked. Modern herbalists value the plant as an astringent and a diuretic. Native peoples often used the stems of mature plants for making string and other cordage material.

Black Henbane

Hyoscyamus niger L.

NIGHTSHADE FAMILY

These plants are imports from Europe that are looked upon as a noxious weed. The plant is a biennial and has large, irregularly shaped, robust leaves, growing to about a metre high. The flowers are bell-shaped and formed in crowded, one-sided spikes near the top of the plant. The petals of the flowers have a distinctive and conspicuous network of purple veins, both inside and outside the petals. The flowers mature to a capsule that contains many seeds and resembles a peanut in shape and texture.

Black Henbane contains a number of poisonous alkaloids that are the same as those produced by Belladonna, including atropine and scopolamine. During the Middle Ages this plant was used in brewing beer to augment the inebriating properties of the product. That practice was eventually abandoned owing to a number of poisonings. Henbane is grown commercially today, and its alkaloids are applied in modern medicine in the production of painkillers and anti-spasmodic drugs.

Blunt-Leaved Bog Orchid

Habenaria obtusata (BANKS EX PURSH) RICH.

(ALSO *Platanthera obtusata*) ORCHID FAMILY

The solitary leaf and small, greenish-white flowers of this bog orchid make it easy to distinguish from other local orchids. The single basal leaf is oblong and blunt on the end, tapering to the sheathing base. The stem grows up to about 20 cm tall, with the flowers distributed up the stem. The flowers have a strap-shaped lip and a tapering spur that is about as long as the lip.

The genus name, *Habenaria*, is from the Latin *habena*, meaning "rein," a reference to the rein-like appendages on the lip. The species name, *obtusata*, means "blunt," a reference to the shape of the single leaf. The species is pollinated by mosquitoes, which are usually in no short supply in the habitat of this lovely orchid.

Heart-Leaved Twayblade

Listera cordata (L.) R. BR.

ORCHID FAMILY

This small orchid, standing about 15 cm high, prefers a cool, damp, mossy habitat. As a consequence of its size and preferred location, it is an easy flower to miss. The white flowers are scattered up the stem in an open raceme. The lip of the flower in this species is deeply split, almost in two. The stem-and-leaf structure of the genus is distinctive, with two leaves appearing opposite to each other partway up the stem.

The common name Twayblade, refers to the two leaves that appear on opposite sides of the stem, about halfway up the stem. The genus name, *Listera*, commemorates Dr. Martin Lister, an English naturalist of the 1600s. The species name, *cordata*, means "heart-shaped," a reference to the shape of the stem leaves.

Hooded Ladies' Tresses
Spiranthes romanzoffiana CHAM.

ORCHID FAMILY

This orchid is reasonably common in the Rocky Mountains and can stand up to 60 cm high. The characteristic feature of the plant is the crowded flower spike, which can contain up to 60 densely spaced, white flowers that appear to coil around the end of the stem in three spiraling ranks. When newly bloomed, the flower has a wonderful aroma, which most people say smells like vanilla.

The common name of the plant is a reference to the braid-like appearance of the flowers, similar to a braid in a lady's hair. The genus name is from the Greek *speira*, meaning "coil," and *anthos*, meaning "flower," referring to the spiral inflorescence. The species name honours Russian Count Nicholas Romanzoff, a 19th-century Russian minister of state and patron of science. The species was first discovered on the Aleutian island of Unalaska, when Alaska was still a Russian territory.

Rattlesnake Plantain
Goodyera oblongifolia RAF.

ORCHID FAMILY

This orchid grows in shaded, dry or moist, coniferous woods in the Rocky Mountains. It is a single-stemmed, stiff, hairy perennial that grows up to 40 cm tall. The basal leaves are distinctive, with a white mottled mid-vein and whitish lateral veins. The robust, downy spike bears small, greenish-white flowers in a loose, one-sided or twisted raceme, with the lower flowers blooming first. The lip of the flower has a wide-open mouth, pressed up against the overhanging hood.

The common name originates from the mottled white markings on the leaves, which reminded early European settlers of the markings on a rattlesnake. Plantain comes from the Latin *planta*, meaning "foot," a reference to the broad, flat, foot-like leaves. The genus name commemorates the 17th-century English botanist John Goodyer.

Round-Leaved Orchid

Amerorchis rotundifolia (BANKS EX PURSH) HULT.

ORCHID FAMILY

This tiny orchid, standing no more than 25 cm tall, occurs in well-drained parts of bogs and swamps, and in cold, moist, mossy, coniferous forests. The flowers are irregular, with three white to pink sepals. The upper sepal combines with the upper two purple-veined petals to form a hood. The two lateral sepals are wing-like. The lowest petal forms a white to pink, oblong lip, spotted with dark red or purple spots. The leaves are basal, solitary, and broadly elliptic.

The genus name is from the Greek *orchis*, meaning "testicle," because the swollen tubers of some species resemble testicles. As a result of this, orchids were once thought to be a powerful aphrodisiac for both people and animals. The species name, *rotundifolia*, is Latin, meaning "round-leafed."

Tall White Bog Orchid

Habenaria dilatata (PURSH) HOOK. (ALSO *Platanthera dilatata*)

ORCHID FAMILY

As the common name suggests, this plant favours wet ground, shaded woods, bogs, pond edges, and streamside environments. It grows up to a metre tall and produces white to greenish, sweet-scented flowers in a spike-like cluster, with flowers distributed along the stalk. The flowers are waxy and small, with the lowest petal forming a lip that widens at the base. The flower also has a slender, curved spur. The lance-shaped leaves are prominently veined and fleshy, short at the base, longest in the middle of the plant and shorter at the top.

The genus name, *Habenaria*, is from the Latin *habena*, meaning "rein," a reference to the rein-like appendages on the lip. The species name, *dilatata*, means "dilated," a reference to the expanded base of the lip on the flower. When blooming, this flower has a heavenly scent, variously described as of vanilla, mock orange, and cloves. Some Native peoples believed the plant to be poisonous to humans and animals, and used an extract from the plant to sprinkle on baits for coyotes and grizzlies.

White Clover (Dutch Clover)
Trifolium repens L.
PEA FAMILY

This common plant was introduced from Eurasia for hay, pasture, and soil improvementi—it being a nitrogen fixer in the soil. The leaves are composed of three leaflets—occasionally four, if you are lucky—and creep along the ground. The flowers are white and clustered on short, slender stalks in round heads. The flower cluster is quite intricate in shape and worthy of close examination.

The name "clover" originates from the Latin *clava*, meaning the three-headed weapon carried by Hercules. That same reference is seen in playing cards—the suit called clubs. Historically, the flowers have been used to flavour cheese and tobacco, and have even been used in famine time to make bread.

White Peavine

Lathyrus ochroleucus HOOK.

PEA FAMILY

A plant of moist, shaded woods and thicket edges, this twining perennial has coiled tendrils at the ends of the leaves, and it climbs on adjacent plants. The flowers are pale yellow to white and pea-like.

Lathyrus is from the ancient Greek name for a plant like this or some other member of the pea family. The species name, *ochroleucus*, is Greek, meaning "yellowish-white," alluding to the flower colour. There is also a purple-flowered Peavine in the same habitat (*L. venosus*). The peavines are distinguished from the vetches by their larger leaves and stipules.

Moss Phlox
Phlox hoodii RICHARDS.

PHLOX FAMILY

A plant of dry, exposed hillsides, eroded slopes, foothills, and prairies.
The small, five-petaled flowers with orange stamens are united into a tube
below. The leaves are awl-shaped with spiny tips, tiny and overlapping,
grey-green, and woolly at the base. The plant grows low to the ground,
and covers the ground like a moss. The flowers show a tremendous variance
in colour, from white to all shades of blue and purple.

The genus name, *Phlox*, is Greek for "flame." The species name, *hoodii*,
honours Robert Hood, a midshipman on one of Sir John Franklin's
expeditions. This flower blooms early in the spring and adds a wonderful
spectrum of colour to an otherwise drab landscape.

Bladder Campion

Silene cucubalus WIBEL.

PINK FAMILY

A plant that was introduced from Eurasia, the Bladder Campion puts down deep roots that allow it to survive on roadsides, gravelly places, and other disturbed areas. The plant is distinctive in that it has an inflated sepal tube, marked by a network of veins. The corolla is formed by five deeply bilobed petals, which spread out like a wheel beyond the rim of the sepal tube.

This plant spreads rapidly and may crowd out desirable native species. The species name, *cucubalus*, is from the Greek *kakos*, meaning "bad," and *bolos*, meaning "a shot," referring to an early belief that this plant was destructive to the soil.

Field Chickweed (Mouse-Ear Chickweed)
Cerastium arvense L.

PINK FAMILY

This early-blooming plant thrives in dry grassland and in rocky and disturbed ground, often forming large mats of white flowers in the spring. The white flowers appear in loose clusters, often many flowers to each plant. The five white petals are notched and have green lines on them as nectar guides for insects.

The upper part of the leaf resembles a mouse's ear, thus the common name for the plant. The genus name, *Cerastium*, is from the Greek *keras*, meaning "horn," a reference to the shape of the seed capsule. The species name, *arvense*, means "field."

Mealy Primrose

Primula incana M.E. JONES

PRIMROSE FAMILY

A plant of moist meadows and slopes, slough margins, and lake margins, these plants grow low to the ground with a basal rosette of leaves. The flowers are pale purple to white, with yellow centers. The petals are deeply notched and appear at the end of a tubular calyx.

The common name refers to the cream-coloured, mealy scales on the undersides of the leaves. *Primula* is from the Latin *primus*, meaning "first," a reference to the early blooming time of many in the genus. The species name, *incana*, is Latin for "pale grey or hoary."

Starflower
Trientalis latifolia HOOK.

PRIMROSE FAMILY

This plant appears at low to mid elevations in shady, moist forests, forest openings, and seepage sites. The small pink to white, saucer-shaped corolla is deeply divided into six or seven sharply pointed lobes. Each flower is borne on a thin, curved stalk that rises from the center of the leaf whorl. The leaves are oval elliptic and emerge in a whorl at the top of a stem that grows low to the ground.

The genus name, *Trientalis*, is Latin for "one-third of a foot," which aptly describes the height of the plant. The common name, Starflower, has been applied because the flowers grow on a very slender stalk, leaving them apparently hanging in the air like tiny stars.

Sweet-Flowered Androsace (Rock Jasmine)
Androsace chamaejasme WULFEN

PRIMROSE FAMILY

This striking, low-growing cushion plant is seldom more than 10 cm tall, but can form mats of flowers on rocky ledges and fields. The flowers are borne on a single, white, hairy stem, and they occur in umbels of four or five flowers. The petals of the flowers are white, with a yellow or orange eye. Though small, the wonderful aroma of these flowers is worth getting down on hands and knees to smell.

The genus name, *Androsace*, is from the Greek *androsakes*, a marine plant. The species name, *chamaejasme*, is from the Greek *chamae*, meaning "dwarf" or "low on the ground," and *jasme*, meaning "jasmine," thus a common name for the plant—Rock Jasmine.

Western Spring Beauty
Claytonia lanceolata PURSH

PURSLANE FAMILY

The flowers of this early-blooming plant are white, but may appear pink, owing to the reddish veins in the petals and the pink anthers. The tips of the petals are distinctly notched. The plants are usually less than 20 cm tall, and the flowers appear in loose, terminal, short-stalked clusters.

The genus name honours John Clayton, a 17th-century botanist who collected plants in what was to become the United States. The species name, *lanceolata*, refers to the lance-shaped leaves. The Western Spring Beauty is in the same family as the Bitterroot (*Lewisia rediviva*) and, like the Bitterroot, was used by Native peoples as food. Bears and rodents also make use of the corms of the plant for food. Ungulates often eat the flowers and leaves.

Birch-Leaf Spirea
Spiraea betulifolia PALL.

ROSE FAMILY

This deciduous shrub grows to heights of 70 cm and occurs in moist to dry, open and wooded sites from valley floors to the subalpine zone. It spreads by underground runners and often forms dense cover on the forest floor. The plant is alternately branched with cinnamon-brown bark and alternate oval or egg-shaped leaves that are irregularly coarse-toothed towards the tip. The flowers are dull white, often tinged to purple or pink, and saucer-shaped, and occur in flat-topped clusters on the ends of the stems.

The genus name, *Spiraea*, is from the Greek *speira*, meaning "spire" or "wreath," possibly a reference to this plant being used as a garland. The species name, *betulifolia*, means "leaves like a birch," the reference being to the similarity of Spirea leaves to those of birch trees. Another common name for the plant is White Meadowsweet. Native peoples and herbalists have long used the plant to relieve pain, reduce inflammations, and treat a variety of other ailments from heartburn to abdominal and menstrual pains. The branches of the plant were also used for drying and smoking fish.

Black Hawthorn
Crataegus douglasii LINDL.

ROSE FAMILY

This is a large, deciduous shrub that can reach up to 8 m in height. The bark is grey, rough, and scaly, and the plant has sharp, stout thorns up to 3 cm long that will command immediate attention from the unwary passerby who stumbles into the plant. The leaves are oval-shaped and appear leathery, with multiple lobes at the top. The flowers are white, showy, and saucer-shaped, occurring in clusters at the tips of the branches. The berries are generally unpalatable, dark purplish pomes that contain a large, hard seed.

The genus name, *Crataegus*, is from the Greek *kratos*, meaning "strength," a reference to the hard, fine-grained wood of the plant. The common name is derived from the Anglo-Saxon word *haguthorn*, which was "a fence with thorns," referring to the use of this plant as a hedge. Native peoples used the thorns from the plant for various purposes, including probing blisters and boils, fish hooks, and piercing ears. The wood of the plant was used for making tool and weapon handles. The bark from the plant was used medicinally by some Native peoples for treatment of diarrhea and stomach pains. Modern herbalists value hawthorn berries as a tonic for the treatment of high blood pressure.

Chokecherry

Prunus virginiana L.

ROSE FAMILY

This plant is a conspicuous, white-flowering shrub or small tree that is common in thickets and open woods, and along streams. The five-petalled, saucer-shaped flowers are borne in thick, cylindrical clusters. The fruit is a red-purple to black berry that is almost all pit. The fruit appears in dense clusters at the terminal ends of branches.

Most people find the fruit of the Chokecherry too bitter to eat raw, thus the common name. The fruits can be processed to produce quite acceptable jelly, syrup, and wine. Birds and mammals seem to relish the fruits. Bears are often drawn to large congregations of chokecherries and will work over the bushes until the chokecherries are gone. Ungulates such as elk and deer forage on the leaves and twigs of the plant.

Saskatoon (Serviceberry)
Amelanchier alnifolia NUTT.

ROSE FAMILY

This deciduous shrub grows to heights of up to five or more metres and is found in open woods, and on streambanks and hillsides from the prairie to montane elevations. The shrub is erect to spreading, with smooth bark that is reddish when new, turning greyish with age. The leaves are alternate, oval to round in shape, rounded at the tips, and coarsely toothed on the upper half. The white flowers are star-shaped with five slender petals, about 2 cm across and occurring in clusters near the branch tips. The petals are wider above the middle and taper to a slender base. The fruits are sweet and juicy, berry-like pomps—like tiny apples—purple to black when ripe.

Saskatoon berries were one of the most important berries for Native peoples. They were eaten fresh or were dried for later use. They were also mashed and dried into large cakes. The Lewis and Clark expedition reported some of these cakes weighed as much as seven kilograms. The dried fruits were often added to meats, soups, and stews. The hard, straight branches of the plant were also used for manufacturing arrow shafts, basket rims, canoe parts, and teepee stakes and closures. The plants are also important browse for elk, moose, and deer, and the berries are eaten by bears, small mammals, and birds. During the Great Depression, the Saskatoon was the only fruit known to thousands of prairie dwellers. Other common names for the plant include Juneberry, Serviceberry and Shadbush.

Thimbleberry
Rubus parviflorus NUTT.

ROSE FAMILY

A plant that often forms thickets on avalanche slopes and the margins of forests and streams. The plant is closely related to the Raspberry, but this vigorous shrub does not have prickles or spines. The plant can grow up to two metres tall. It has large leaves, each with three to five lobes with jagged-toothed margins, resembling a maple leaf in shape. The flowers are white, with a central core of yellow stamens. There are usually three to five flowers in clusters at the ends of branches. The bright red fruit looks like a flattened Raspberry, but it is rather tasteless and very seedy.

Native peoples peeled the young shoots of Thimbleberry and ate it raw or cooked with meat in stews. The large leaves were widely used as temporary containers, to line baskets, and to separate items in the same basket. They also make a good biodegradable toilet tissue substitute when needed.

Trailing Raspberry
Rubus pubescens RAF.
ROSE FAMILY

This dwarf shrub is a low, trailing plant with slender runners and erect, flowering stems that grows at low to mid elevations in moist to wet forests and clearings. The plant has soft hairs, but no prickles like the Wild Red Raspberry (*R. idaeus*). The leaves are palmately divided into three oval or diamond-shaped leaflets with pointed tips and toothed margins. The flowers are white and spreading, and occur on short, erect branches. The fruits are red drupelets—clusters that make up a raspberry.

Native peoples used this plant as a food source and for medicinal purposes, similarly to the Wild Red Raspberry (*R. idaeus*).

Western Mountain Ash

Sorbus scopulina GREENE

ROSE FAMILY

This deciduous, erect to spreading shrub grows to heights of four metres in moist, open or shaded places from the foothills to the subalpine zones. The branches are slightly white, hairy, and sticky when new; reddish-grey to yellowish when mature. The leaves are alternate and pinnately compound—leaflets appearing opposite each other on both sides of a common axis—with 11 to 13 leaflets per leaf. The leaflets are sharply tipped and sharply toothed from tip to base. The flowers are white and saucer-shaped, with five broad petals, and they occur in large, flat-topped clusters. The fruits are glossy orange to red, berry-like pomes in dense clusters.

Some Native peoples ate the pomes of this plant, but most looked upon them as inedible. Some tribes boiled the peeled branches or inner bark of the plant to make medicinal concoctions. The plant is used quite extensively as a garden ornamental. The fruit clusters are a favoured food of a variety of bird species.

White Cinquefoil
Potentilla arguta L.

ROSE FAMILY

This species of Cinquefoil is tall—up to 100 cm—and bears creamy-white flowers in a compact flower arrangement. It is a glandular, hairy plant that appears in grasslands and meadows.

The genus name, *Potentilla*, comes from the Latin *potens*, meaning "powerful," most probably a reference to the potent medicinal properties of some of the herbs in the genus. Potentillas have a high tannin content, making them astringent and anti-inflammatory. Herbalists use the plants in the genus for a wide variety of conditions.

Wild Red Raspberry

Rubus idaeus L.

ROSE FAMILY

This erect to spreading deciduous shrub grows up to two metres tall at low to subalpine elevations in clearings, along streams, and in disturbed areas. It is similar to cultivated Raspberry in appearance. The prickly branches (or canes) are biennial, and are green in the first year and yellowish-brown to cinnamon-brown in the second. The leaves are palmately divided (i.e. divided into leaflets that diverge from a common point) into three to five egg-shaped, pointed, double-saw-toothed leaflets. The flowers are white and drooping, occurring singly or in small clusters. The fruits are juicy, red drupelets—a drupelet being one part of an aggregate fruit—in dense clusters, the totality of which is the raspberry. Other examples of fruits that appear as drupelets include Blackberries and Thimbleberries.

Native peoples made extensive use of Wild Red Raspberries as a food source and for medicinal purposes. A tea brewed from the plant was administered to women to ease the pain of childbirth, and the concoction was also used to treat a variety of other conditions, such as boils, bladder infections, liver problems, and diarrhea. Modern herbalists also value this plant for a variety of conditions. Pharmacologists have validated raspberry leaf as an anti-spasmodic.

Wild Strawberry
Fragaria virginiana DUCHN.

ROSE FAMILY

A plant of shaded to open, gravelly soils and thickets from prairie to alpine habitats. The single, five-petaled, white flower appears on a leafless stem that is usually shorter than the leaves are long. The stamens are numerous and yellow. The leaves are rounded to broadly oval, toothed, with three leaflets on short stalks. The fruit is a red berry, covered with sunken, seed-like achenes. New plants are often established from reddish runners.

Strawberry is said to come from the Anglo-Saxon name *streowberie* because the runners from the plant are strewn across the ground. The genus name, *Fragaria*, means "fragrance." Strawberry plants are rich in iron, calcium, potassium, sodium, and vitamin C. The fruits are delicious, with a more pronounced flavour than domestic strawberries. The leaves have been used to make tea and have also been used for medicinal purposes.

Pale Comandra (Bastard Toadflax)
Comandra umbellata (L.) NUTT.

SANDALWOOD FAMILY

This erect, blue-green perennial is common in open pine woods, gravel slopes, and grasslands, and springs from a creeping rootstalk. The leaves are lance-shaped and hug the erect stem. The flowers occur in a rounded or flat-topped cluster atop the stem. Each flower is greenish-white, with the sepals separated above and fused into a small funnel below.

The genus name, *Comandra*, is from the Greek *kome*, meaning "hair," and *andros*, meaning "man," probably a reference to the hairy bases of the stamens on the flower. The species name, *umbellata*, is a reference to the shape of the cluster of flowers. The plant has another common name—Bastard Toadflax—though the plant bears no relationship to Toadflax and is not in any way similar. Pale Comandra is a parasite, taking water, and perhaps food, from its host plant.

Foamflower
Tiarella trifoliata L.

SAXIFRAGE FAMILY

These beautiful flowers inhabit moist, coniferous woods, streambanks, and trails in the boreal forest. The plant grows up to 50 cm in height, and the flowers are white or pinkish, arranged in open panicles well above the leaves. The leaves are compound, usually with three leaflets. The middle leaflet is usually three-lobed and three-toothed.

The genus name, *Tiarella*, is from the Latin *tiara*, an ancient Persian turban-like headdress. The species name, *trifoliata*, refers to the compound leaf with three leaflets. Other common names applied to the plant are Laceflower and False Mitrewort.

Small-Flowered Woodland Star

Lithophragma parviflorum (HOOK.) NUTT.

SAXIFRAGE FAMILY

This perennial grows up to 30 cm tall and occurs in low elevation grasslands, open Ponderosa Pine stands, and Sagebrush areas. It blooms early in the spring. The leaves are mostly basal, kidney-shaped with deeply cleft and divided blades. The flowers are white to pinkish, and occur in clusters at the tip of the stem. The flowers are broadly funnel-shaped, with five spreading, deeply lobed petals.

The genus name, *Lithophragma*, is puzzling. It comes from the Greek *lithos*, meaning "stone," and *phragma*, meaning "wall," suggesting a habitat different to that where the plant appears. Another common name for this plant is Fringe-Cup, referring to the deeply cleft petals that are so deeply cleft that it almost appears as if the flower is fringed. Woodland Star flowers resemble Mouse-Ear Chickweed (*Cerastium arvense*), but the petals of the former are notched in threes, where the latter are notched in twos.

Round-Leaved Alumroot
Heuchera cylindrica DOUGL.

DAXIFRAGE FAMILY

This robust perennial can grow to heights approaching a metre, and can be widespread and common on dry plateaus, open forests, and rocky outcrops. The leaves are all basal and are heart- or kidney-shaped. The cream to greenish-yellow flowers are somewhat bell-shaped and grouped at the top of a tall, thin, leafless stem. The flowers have a decidedly hairy appearance.

The Alumroots were important for medicinal purposes for Native peoples. It works as a styptic for stopping bleeding and closing wounds. These plants are still used by herbalists. The root of the plant is a very intense astringent (like alum), thus the common name for the plant. The genus name, *Heuchera*, is to honour Johann Heinrich von Heucher, an 18th-century German botanist and physician. Alumroot is also used as a mordant to fix dyes, and many people prefer it to the manufactured alternatives.

Spotted Saxifrage
Saxifraga bronchialis L.

SAXIFRAGE FAMILY

These beautiful flowers inhabit rocky crevices, rock faces, screes, and open slopes, often appearing as if by magic from the rocks. The white flowers appear in clusters at the top of the wiry, brown stems, and have small, red or yellow spots near the tips of the five petals. A close examination of this beautiful flower is well worth the time.

The genus name, *Saxifraga*, is from the Latin *saxum*, meaning "rock," and *frangere*, meaning "to break," a reference to the fact that the Saxifrages usually grow on rocks and are thought to be capable of breaking rocks into soil. The species name, *bronchialis*, is from the Latin *bronchus*, meaning "branch" or "division," a reference to the branching, mat-like growth of the plant.

Sitka Valerian
Valeriana sitchensis BONG.

VALERIAN FAMILY

This perennial grows up to 80 cm tall and has a somewhat succulent, squarish stem. It occurs in moist subalpine and alpine environments, in alpine meadows, and along streams. The leaves are large and opposite, divided into three to seven coarsely toothed lobes, with progressively shorter petioles up the stem. The numerous tubular flowers are crowded into a nearly flat-topped cluster at the top of the stem. The buds and young flowers are a pale lavender colour, but the flowers later fade to white. The floral tubes are notched into five equal lobes.

There appear to be two schools of thought as to where this genus gets its name. One school opines that the genus name is derived from Valeria, a Roman province in southern Europe, now a part of Hungary. The other school contends that the genus name comes from the Latin *valere*, meaning "to be healthy," a reference to the fact that the plant has long been used for various medicinal purposes. The species name, *sitchensis*, is from Sitka Sound in southeastern Alaska, where the species was first collected and described. Two common names for the plant are Wild Heliotrope and Tobacco Root. The Tobacco Root Range in Montana takes its name from the plant. Valerian is the original source of diazepam, a tranquilizer and muscle relaxant commonly known as Valium.

Western Canada Violet

Viola canadensis L.

VIOLET FAMILY

This plant favours moist to fairly dry, deciduous forests, floodplains, and clearings. The flowers are held on aerial stems and are white with yellow bases. The lower three petals have purple lines, and the upper two have a purplish tinge on the back. The leaves are heart-shaped, long-stalked, and decidedly pointed at the tip, and have saw-toothed edges. This small, white flower splashes shady woods and marshes in the midsummer.

The plant grows from short, thick rhizomes with slender, creeping runners with leafy aerial stems. These violets are easily propagated from runners or sections of rhizomes and can be invasive in a garden setting. Violet flowers have long been used as a poultice for swellings.

Blue and Purple Flowers

This section includes flowers that are predominantly blue or purple when encountered in the field—ranging from pale blue to deep purple, light violet to lavender. Some of the lighter colours of blue and purple might shade into pinks, so if you do not find the flower you are looking for here, check the other sections of this book.

Common Hound's-Tongue
Cynoglossum officinale L.

BORAGE FAMILY

This course, hairy, biennial weed was introduced from Europe and grows in disturbed ground and roadside ditches. It has a single, leafy stem that grows to 80 cm in height. The leaves are alternate, elliptic to lance-shaped, tapered to slender stalks at the base of the plant and becoming stalkless and clasping near the top of the plant. The flowers are reddish-purple and funnel-shaped with five spreading lobes. The flowers appear from the upper leaf axils. The fruits are clusters of small nutlets that are covered with barbed prickles.

The genus name, *Cynoglossum*, is from the Greek *cynos*, meaning "dog," and *glossa*, meaning "tongue." The hooked spines on the fruits catch on clothing and fur, a mechanism for seed distribution. Some people experience skin irritation when they come into contact with the plant. In the words of the famous naturalist Lewis J. Clark: "The plant is coarse and unattractive."

Forget-Me-Not
Myosotis laxa LEHM.

BORAGE FAMILY

This beautiful little flower is easily recognized by its wheel-shaped, blue corolla and its prominent yellow eye. This plant occurs at lower elevations in moist habitats. The Alpine Forget-Me-Not is very similar, though smaller. Alpine Forget-Me-Not is the state flower of Alaska.

The genus name, *Myosotis*, is from the Greek *mus*, meaning "mouse," and *ous*, meaning "ear," descriptive of the short, furred leaves of some species. The species name, *laxa*, means "open" or "loose," probably a reference to the sprawling plant structure. There seems to be some dispute as to the origin of the common name. One school of thought holds that the name dates back to the 1500s when a blue flower was traditionally worn to retain a lover's affections. Another school of thought holds that a couple was walking along the Danube River, and the woman remarked on the beauty of some blue flowers blooming on a steep slope by the river. The man attempted to fetch the flowers for his sweetheart, but fell into the river, asking her as he fell to "forget me not."

Mertensia (Low Lungwort)
Mertensia oblongifolia (NUTT.) G. DON.

BORAGE FAMILY

This plant of the sagebrush flats and open Ponderosa pines blooms early in the spring, and the flower resembles oblong bluebells. The plants grow very near to the ground, with the flowers hanging down in clusters, first looking like oblong blue capsules, then opening to be oblong, blue, bell-shaped flowers.

The genus name, *Mertensia*, honours F.C. Mertens, an early German botanist. The common name, Lungwort is derived from Europe, this plant's flowers being similar to the European Lungwort, a plant thought to be good in the treatment of lung diseases. A related species—Tall Lungwort (*M. paniculata*)—is a much larger plant overall, growing from a woody rootstock and almost resembling a shrub. It occurs in moister habitat in meadows and woods. The flowers are very similar to Low Lungwort. Montana Bluebell is another common name that seems to be shared by all of the Mertensias.

Blueweed

Echium vulgare L.

BORAGE FAMILY

This European import is found in roadsides, pastures, and disturbed areas throughout Canada, and is becoming a problem weed, forcing out native vegetation. The flowers are a spectacular bright blue, funnel-shaped, with unequal lobes. The flowers are distributed up a central stalk that can reach over a metre in height. The plant has an overall hairy appearance.

Blueweed is also known as Viper's Bugloss and Blue Devil. At one time the plant was believed to be useful in treating snakebite. In addition, the seed shape resembles a viper's head, hence the reference to viper. Bugloss is from the Greek *bous*, meaning "ox," and *glossa*, meaning "tongue," the reference being that the rough leaves of this plant resemble the tongue of an ox. The genus name, *Echium*, is from the Greek *echis*, meaning "viper," most probably a reference to the shape of the seed of the plant. The bristly hairs on the leaves and stem of the plant cause severe skin irritation.

Western Stickseed

Hackelia floribunda (LEHM.) JOHNST.

BORAGE FAMILY

This plant is a hairy biennial or short-lived perennial that has stiffly erect stems and grows to a metre tall. The flowers are small, yellow-centered, blue flowers that occur in loose clusters on curving stalks near the top of the plant. The nutlets produced are keeled in the middle, attached to a pyramid-shaped base. Each nutlet has rows of barbed prickles.

While the flowers on this plant are lovely to look at, the prickles on the nutlets cling easily to fur, feathers, and clothing, thus lending the plant its common name. The nutlets adhere to clothing like Velcro and can be a huge nuisance in the late summer and autumn to anybody who walks close to the plant. The nutlets are tenacious and must be labouriously picked from socks, sweaters, and trousers. Long-haired hunting dogs can become covered in the nutlets, even to the extent that scissors are required to free the animal of the things. The nutlets are an extraordinarily effective mechanism for seed dispersal.

Blue Clematis
Clematis occidentalis (HORNEM.) DC.

BUTTERCUP FAMILY

A plant of shaded riverine woods and thickets, the Clematis is a climbing, slightly hairy, reddish-stemmed vine that attaches itself to other plants by slender tendrils. The flowers have four to five sepals, purplish to blue in colour, with dark veins. The flowers resemble crepe paper.

The common name is derived from the Greek word *klema*, meaning "vine branch or tendril." The Blackfoot called the plant Ghost's Lariat, a reference to the fact that the vine would entangle their feet when they walked through it. Many tribes used the plant to weave mats and bags. The whole plant is toxic if ingested. Clematis also occurs in yellow (*C. tangutica*) and white (*C. ligusticifolia*), and often goes by the locally common name of Virgin's Bower.

Blue Columbine
Aquilegia brevistyla HOOK.

BUTTERCUP FAMILY

This plant occurs in deciduous, coniferous, and mixed woods, meadows, and riverine environments, and grows to heights of 80 cm. It has slender, slightly purplish, hairy stems. The attractive flower can be nodding or ascending, with yellowish or white petals and five blue to purplish, reflexed sepals. The bluish-green leaflets with scalloped tips appear in threes. Columbines have a very distinctive floral structure and are usually unmistakable when seen.

The name Columbine is derived from the Latin *columbina*, meaning "dove-like," it being said that the petals resemble a group of doves drinking at a dish. The origin of the genus name, *Aquilegia*, is fraught with some uncertainty. One school of thought attributes the name to the Latin *aquila*, meaning "eagle," a reference to the long, claw-like spur on the flower supposedly resembling an eagle's talon. The other school of thought is that the name comes from *aqua*, meaning "water" and *legere*, meaning "to collect," as little drops of nectar collect at the ends of the spurs. An interesting juxtaposition, with the war symbol eagle on one side, and the peace symbol dove on the other. Bumblebees and butterflies are drawn to the Columbines to collect the nectar. Columbines also appear in western North America in yellow (*A. flavescens*) and red (*A. formosa*).

Low Larkspur
Delphinium bicolor NUTT.

BUTTERCUP FAMILY

A plant of open woods, grasslands, and slopes, Larkspurs are easily recognized for their showy, highly modified flowers. The irregular petals are whitish to bluish, with sepals that are blue to violet. The upper sepal forms a large, hollow, nectar-producing spur. The flowers bloom up the stem in a loose, elongated cluster.

The genus name, *Delphinium*, is derived from the Greek word *delphin*, which means "dolphin," as the plant's nectaries are said to resemble old pictures of dolphins. The common name is said to have originated because the spur on the flower resembled the spur on the foot of a lark. The flowers are favoured by bumblebees and butterflies. The plant contains delphinine, a toxic alkaloid, and is poisonous to cattle and humans.

Monkshood

Aconitum delphinifolium DC.

BUTTERCUP FAMILY

A plant of moist mixed and coniferous forests and meadows, Monkshood has a distinctive flower construction that is unmistakable when encountered. The dark blue to purple flowers appear in terminal clusters, and the sepals form a hood like those worn by monks.

The genus name, *Aconitum*, is from the Greek *acon*, meaning "dart," a reference to the fact that arrows were often tipped with poison from this plant, the entire plant being poisonous. The plant contains alkaloids that can cause paralysis, decreased blood pressure, and temperature, and can cause death within a few hours.

Prairie Crocus

Pulsatilla patens (L.) P. MILL SSP. *multifida* (PRITZ.) ZAMELS

(FORMERLY KNOWN AS *Anemone patens*) BUTTERCUP FAMILY

This plant is widespread and common in grasslands, dry meadows, and mountain slopes. It is usually one of the first wildflowers to bloom in the spring and can occur in huge numbers. The flowers are usually solitary, various blues to purples in colour, and cup-shaped. White varieties are sometimes seen. It is interesting to note that the flower blooms before the basal leaves appear. The plant has many basal leaves, palmately divided into three main leaflets and again divided into narrow, linear segments. The leaves on the flower stem appear in a whorl of three. The fruits are large, spherical clusters of silky-haired, long-plumed seeds that are distributed by the wind.

The Prairie Crocus is also known as a Pasque Flower, "pasque" being an old French word for Easter and referencing the blooming of this flower around the time of Easter. The texture of the petals is as soft as down. Prairie Crocus is the floral emblem of Manitoba. The origin of the genus name, *Anemone*, is uncertain, but it is believed to come from the Greek word *anemos*, which means "wind," most probably a reference to the fact that the wind distributes the seeds of the plant. Prairie Crocus, like many of the Anemones, contains a substance called protoanemonin, an irritant that can produce rashes.

Fern-Leaved Desert Parsley

Lomatium dissectum (NUTT.) MATH. AND CONST.

CARROT FAMILY

This large plant has several stout, smooth, hairless stems and grows to heights of over a metre in dry, rocky places. The leaves are large (up to 30 cm), finely dissected, and fern-like, and have a spicy aroma. The surface of the leaves has a covering of fine hairs, making it rough to the touch. The flowers are compound umbels of yellow or deep purple sitting atop the ends of the stems. The fruits are elliptic seeds with flattened backs and corky, thick-winged margins.

The genus name, *Lomatium*, comes from the Greek *loma*, meaning "a border," most probably a reference to the winged or ribbed fruit of most of the members of the family. All members of the genus are edible. The specific name, *dissectum*, describes the finely dissected foliage. Meriwether Lewis collected a specimen of the plant in Idaho in 1806 and labelled it: "A great horse medicine among the Natives." Another common name for the plant is Chocolate Tips, a reference to the often purplish-chocolate flowers.

Blue Lettuce

Lactuca tatarica (L.) C.A. MEY. SSP. *pulchella* (PURSH) STEBB.

COMPOSITE FAMILY

A plant of fields, roadsides, meadows, shores, and streambanks, often found on moist, heavy soil. The flowers have pale to dark blue ray florets, toothed at the tip. There are no disk florets. The leaves are hairless, lobed below and simple above.

The genus name, *Lactuca*, is from the Latin *lac*, meaning "milk," and refers to the milky sap from the plant. Plants of this genus are particularly enjoyed by horses apparently, and they are sometimes referred to as Horseweeds.

Blue Sailor
Cichorium intybus L.

COMPOSITE FAMILY

This native of Eurasia grows at low elevations on dry plateaus, fields, grasslands, and waste areas. The flower has sky-blue ray flowers and no disk flowers. The flowers open only in the daylight and burst forth in widely spaced heads on long branches from the bases of stem leaves. Basal leaves are strongly toothed to lobed.

Also known as Chicory and called Belgian Endive in the commercial vegetable trade. The leaves of this plant are eaten as a salad green, a practice dating back to the ancient Egyptians. Chicory and the genus name come from the original Arabic name for wild chicory. The species name, *intybus*, is Latin, meaning "endive."

Bull Thistle
Cirsium vulgare <small>(SAVI)</small> TEN.

COMPOSITE FAMILY

A Eurasian weed introduced to North America that is common in pastures, waste places, clearings, and roadsides. The flowers are large, composite heads with purple disk flowers and no ray flowers. The flower heads are bulbous and covered in sharp spikes. The flower structure is extraordinarily intricate when examined closely. The leaves, both basal and stem, are lance-shaped, deeply lobed, and spiny, clasping the stem. The Bull Thistle will grow to heights of over two metres and will produce a multitude of flowers.

All thistles have spines on their leaf edges, but the Bull Thistle is the only one with a spiny leaf surface. The flowers are a favourite of bees and butterflies. The thistle generally is the national emblem of Scotland, legend having it that a soldier in an invading Danish army stepped on a thistle and cried out in pain, awaking and alerting the Scottish encampment who rose and repelled the invading army. The thistle was thereafter considered to be the guardian of Scotland. Bull Thistle also is known locally as Spear Thistle.

Canada Thistle
Cirsium arvense (L.) SCOPOLI.

COMPOSITE FAMILY

Despite the common name, this noxious weed was introduced to North America from Eurasia. The plant grows to over a metre in height from a thin, white, creeping rhyzome. The flowers occur in heads at the tops of the multiple branches. The flowers are usually pinkish to mauve, but they may be white. The leaves are alternate and oblong to lance-shaped, with wavy margins.

The species name of this plant, *arvense*, means "of cultivated fields," and the plant certainly lives up to its name. By combining a creeping rhyzome and tremendous seed distribution, the plant will quickly take over areas where it grows. If the rhyzome is cut or broken by farming machinery, the spread of the plant is exacerbated. Canada Thistle is dioecious—that is, male and female flowers occur on separate plants.

Common Burdock

Arctium minus (HILL) BERNH.

COMPOSITE FAMILY

A plant of pastures, roadsides, fencerows, and disturbed sites, Common Burdock is erect, with spreading branches, and grows to over a metre in height. The flowers appear at the ends of the branches as purplish to pinkish tubular protrusions with disk florets only. The outer bracts are decidedly hooked at the ends and form a ball around the inflorescence, making the plant appear to be furry and unkempt.

Arctium species are native to and widespread in Eurasia. In Japan the edible roots of the plants are known as *gobo*. It is said that the hooks on the involucral bracts of this plant inspired the creation of Velcro. These hooks are extraordinarily efficient in disseminating the seeds of the plant, clinging as they do to fur on animals and clothing on humans who encounter the plant in the field.

Showy Aster

Aster conspicuus LINDL.

COMPOSITE FAMILY

This plant is widespread and common in low to mid elevations in moist to dry, open forests, openings, clearings, and meadows. The flowers are few to many composite heads on glandular stalks, with 15 to 35 violet ray flowers and yellow disk flowers. The stem leaves are egg-shaped to elliptical with sharp-toothed edges and clasping bases.

Aster is the Latin name for "star," referring to the flower's shape. *Conspicuus* means "conspicuous," a reference to the showy flowers. Some Native peoples soaked the roots of the plant in water and used the liquid to treat boils. The leaves were also used as a poultice for that purpose.

Smooth Blue Aster

Aster laevis L.

COMPOSITE FAMILY

This plant inhabits open wooded areas, meadows, coulees, and ditches, often on gravelly soil. The plants are erect, up to 120 cm tall, and can form large colonies. The flowers are composed of pale to dark purple or bluish ray florets, surrounding bright yellow disk florets.

The genus name, *Aster*, is from the Latin for "star," a reference to the general shape of the flower. Smooth Blue Aster is believed to be a selenium absorber, and therefore dangerous to livestock who consume it. Selenium is cumulative in the system, and too much can lead to symptoms such as the blind staggers.

Blue-Eyed Mary

Collinsia parviflora LINDL.

FIGWORT FAMILY

This small annual grows in moist to dry, shaded or open sites from the foothills to the montane zone. The branched stems are slender and weak, causing the plant to sprawl. The leaves are opposite, narrowly egg-shaped to linear, and tapered to the base and tip. The upper leaves often appear in whorls of three to five leaflets. The small flowers are pale blue, to white and blue and emerge from the axils of the upper leaves. The flowers are similar in shape to violets, with two lips. The upper lip has two lobes and the lower has three, with the middle lobe being folded inwards.

These flowers are early bloomers and often appear where other plants are sparse. The genus name, *Collinsia*, honours Zacheus Collins, an early American botanist. The species name, *parviflora*, is from the Latin, *parvus*, meaning "small," and *flos*, meaning "flower." Blue Lips is another common name for the plant.

Creeping Beardtongue

Penstemon ellipticus COULT. AND FISCH.

FIGWORT FAMILY

One of the most handsome and conspicuous of the Penstemons, Creeping Beardtongue has large, lavender-coloured flowers that seem out of proportion to the low-growing plant. The plant grows in rocky crevices, on taluses, and on cliffs in the subalpine and alpine regions. When in bloom the flowers spill forth in amazing numbers, covering the leaves beneath in a blue-purple flood of colour.

The species name, *ellipticus*, refers to the leaves, which are egg-shaped or oblong with rounded ends. In the spring of the year the beautiful flowers festoon rocky outcrops along trails. The plant is also known by the very appropriate common name Rockvine Beardtongue, given its native habitat.

Shrubby Penstemon

Penstemon fruticosus (PURSH) GREENE

FIGWORT FAMILY

This Beardtongue grows in dry areas from the montane to the subalpine zones. It has woody stems and almost appears to be a shrub, growing to 40 cm in height, hence the common name. The leaves are opposite, lance-shaped, shiny, and evergreen, with the largest leaves appearing at the base of the stem. The flowers are large and lavender to purplish-blue in colour. The flowers appear in pairs on one side of the stem in a raceme.

Native peoples often added the leaves and flowers of this plant to cooking pits to flavour wild onions and balsamroot. The long, tubular flowers are often pollinated by bees and hummingbirds. Meriwether Lewis collected a specimen of this plant in 1806 along the Lolo Trail in Idaho on the return of the party from wintering on the Columbia River.

Small-Flowered Penstemon (Small Flowered Beardtongue)
Penstemon procerus DOUGL.

FIGWORT FAMILY

This plant grows to heights of 40 cm from low to alpine elevations, usually in dry to moist open forests, grassy clearings, meadows, and disturbed areas. Most of the blunt to lance-shaped leaves appear in opposite pairs up the stem. The flowers are small, funnel-shaped, and blue to purple, and appear in one to several tight clusters arranged in whorls around the stem and at its tip.

The genus name, *Penstemon*, is from the Greek *penta*, meaning "five," and *stemon*, meaning "thread," a reference to the five thread-like stamens common to the family. The genus is a large and complex group of plants. There are dozens of Penstemons in the Rocky Mountains, and many will hybridize freely, adding even more confusion to the specific identification. Small-Flowered Penstemon can usually be identified by its small, tightly packed flowers that appear in whorls around the stem. Another common Penstemon in the same habitat is Yellow Penstemon (*P. confertus*), which has a similar flower construction with yellow flowers. Two other common names applied to Small-Flowered Penstemon are Slender Beardtongue and Small Flowered Beardtongue. The common name Beardtongue, is applied to the Penstemons because the flowers have "hairs" in the throat of the flower, thus a "bearded tongue."

Taper-Leaved Beardtongue

Penstemon attenuatus DOUGL.

FIGWORT FAMILY

The flowers on this plant are clustered and up to 2 cm long. They can vary in colour from blue to purple to pink. The leaves are lance-shaped and smooth on the margins.

The common name, Beardtongue, describes the hairy, tongue-like staminode (sterile stamen) in the throat of the flower. The genus name, *Penstemon*, originates from the Greek *pente*, meaning "five," and *stemon*, meaning "stamen," five being the total number of stamens in the flower. A number of Penstemons appear in the Rocky Mountains.

Blue Flax

Linum perenne L., ssp. *lewisii* (Purch) Hult.

FLAX FAMILY

A plant of dry, exposed hillsides, grasslands, roadsides, and gravelly river flats. The five-petalled flowers are pale purplish-blue, with darkish guidelines, yellowish at the base. The leaves are alternate, simple, and stalkless. The flowers appear on very slender stems and are constantly moving, even with the smallest of breezes.

The genus name, *Linum*, is from the Greek *linon*, meaning "thread." Each bud of this delicate flower blooms for only one day. The plant has been cultivated for various uses, notably oil and linen, since ancient times.

Northern Gentian

Gentianella amarella (L.) BOERNER SSP. *acuta* (MICHX.) GILLETT.

(ALSO *Gentiana amarella*) GENTIAN FAMILY

A plant of moist places in meadows, moist woods, ditches, and streambanks, these lovely flowers are first sighted by their star-like formation winking at the top of the corolla tube amidst adjacent grasses. The plant is most often small, standing only 15 to 20 cm, though taller specimens are sometimes seen. The flowers appear in clusters in the axils of the upper stem leaves, the leaves being opposite and appearing almost to be small hands holding up the flowers for inspection.

The genus name, *Gentianella*, comes from Gentius, a king of ancient Ilyria, a coastal region on the Adriatic Sea. Gentius was said to have discovered medicinal properties in the plants of this genus. The species name, *amarella*, is from the Latin *amarus*, meaning "bitter," a reference to the bitter alkaloids contained in the plant"s juices. *Acuta* means "sharp-pointed," a reference to the leaves of the plant. The plant is also commonly referred to as Felwort.

Sticky Purple Geranium
Geranium viscosissimum FISCH. AND MEY. EX MEY.

GERANIUM FAMILY

A plant of moist grasslands, open woods, and thickets. The plants can grow up to 60 cm tall. The flowers have large, showy, rose-purple to bluish petals that are strongly veined with purple. The long-stalked leaves are deeply lobed and split into five to seven sharply toothed divisions, appearing in opposite pairs along the stem. There are sticky, glandular hairs covering the stems, leaves, and some flower parts. The fruit is an elongated, glandular, hairy capsule with a long beak shaped like a stork's or crane's bill.

The genus name, *Geranium*, is from the Greek, *geranos*, meaning "crane," a reference to the fruit being shaped like a crane's bill. Indeed, Crane's Bill is an oft-used common name for the Geraniums. The species name, *viscosissimum*, is the Latin superlative for *viscid*, which means "thick and gluey." The sticky, glandular hairs appearing on the stems and leaves effectively protect the plant from pollen theft by ants and other crawling insects. The Sticky Purple Geranium is very similar to a European import that has naturalized in dry grasslands in western North America—the Stork's Bill (*Erodium cicutarium*). Interestingly enough, *Erodium* is Greek for "heron," another bird with a long, pointed bill. The ornithological references to storks, herons, and cranes can certainly lend some confusion when common names are applied to wildflowers of the Geranium (*Geraniaceae*) family.

213

Harebell
Campanula rotundifolia L.

HAREBELL FAMILY

This plant is widespread in a variety of habitats, including grasslands, gullies, moist forests, openings, clearings, and rocky, open ground. The flowers are purplish, blue, rarely white, bell-shaped, with hairless sepals, nodding on a thin stem in loose clusters. The leaves are thin on the stem and lance-shaped. The basal leaves are heart-shaped and coarsely toothed, but they usually wither before the flowers appear.

The genus name, *Campanula*, is from the Latin *campana*, meaning "bell." *Campanula* is the diminutive of *campana*, thus "little bell." The species name, *rotundifolia*, refers to the round basal leaves. This is the Bluebell of Scotland, and one school of thought holds that Harebell comes from a contraction of "heatherbell." Another school of thought holds that "harebell" is a misspelling of "hairbell," the reference being to the hair-thin stems on which the flowers appear. Where Harebells occur, they can be in profusion and can cast a purple hue to the area when they are in bloom. The Cree were said to have chopped and dried the roots to make into compresses for stopping bleeding and to reduce swelling. The foliage contains alkaloids and is avoided by browsing animals.

Blue-Eyed Grass
Sisyrinchium montanum GREENE

IRIS FAMILY

These beautiful flowers are in the Iris family and can be found scattered among the grasses of moist meadows from low to mid elevations. The distinctively flattened stems grow to heights of up to 30 cm and are twice as tall as the grass-like basal leaves. The blue flower is star-shaped, with three virtually identical petals and sepals, each tipped with a minute point. There is a bright yellow eye in the centre of the flower. The blossoms are very short-lived, wilting usually within one day, to be replaced by fresh ones on the succeeding day.

The genus name, *Sisyrinchium*, was a name applied by Theophrastus, a disciple of Aristotle who refined the philosopher"s work in botany and natural sciences in ancient Greece. It is a reference to a plant allied to the Iris. The species name, *montanum*, means "of the mountains." The flower has a number of locally common names, including Montana Blue-Eyed Grass, Idaho Blue-Eyed Grass, Eyebright, Grass Widow and Blue Star.

Wild Chives
Allium shoenoprasum L.

LILY FAMILY

Allium is the Latin name for garlic and designates all wild onions.
Wild Chives grow in wet meadows, along streambanks, and at lake edges.
The small pink or purple flowers are upright on the top of a leafless stalk
and are arranged in a densely packed ball. Wild Chives have round, hollow
leaves near the base and produce a very distinctive "oniony" odour when
broken.

Native peoples harvested wild onion bulbs before the plants flowered and
used the bulbs as food, both raw and cooked. The bulbs were also used for
flavouring other foods such as salmon and meat. Crushed onion bulbs were
also used as a disinfectant and as a poultice to alleviate pain and swelling
from insect bites.

Giant Hyssop
Agastache foeniculum (PURSH) KTZE.

MINT FAMILY

A plant common in thickets and along streams, this member of the mint family is erect and grows to heights of up to 100 cm. The stem is square in cross-section, typical of the Mint family. The leaves are opposite, oval in shape, coarsely toothed, with pointed tips. The blue to purple flowers are densely packed and appear in interrupted clusters along the top of the stem.

The genus name, *Agastache*, is from the Greek *agan*, meaning "much," and *stachys*, meaning "spike," a reference to the way the flowers appear on the top of the stem. The species name, *foeniculum*, means "scent like fennel." Native peoples used the leaves of the plant for making a tea and as a flavouring in foods. The flowers were often collected for medicine bundles.

Heal-All (Self-Heal)

Prunella vulgaris L. ssp *lanceolata* (BART.) HULT.

MINT FAMILY

A plant of moist woods, streambanks, fields, and lakeshores. The flowers occur in terminal clusters, usually surrounded by the upper leaves. The bracts are kidney-shaped to oval, with spines at the tips and hairs along the margins. The few leaves are opposite, smooth, and sparsely hairy. The plant is small and sprawling, and square-stemmed.

The name *Prunella* is most likely derived from the German *Braune*, meaning "quinsy" or "angina," which this plant was used to cure. The traditional use of this plant for healing internal and external bleeding gives rise to the common name. Tests on the plant"s extracts have not revealed any biochemical basis for the claims of healing. Parts of this small flower have been used by Native peoples to relieve boils, cuts, bruises, internal bleeding, and swellings. The Cree treated sore throats with Heal-All. The Blackfoot used it as an eyewash and treated horses" saddle sores with it. The leaves can be brewed into a tea.

Marsh Hedge-Nettle

Stachys palustris L. SSP. *pilosa* (NUTT.) EPLING

MINT FAMILY

A plant of wetland margins, streambanks, marshes, and wet ditches, Marsh Hedge-Nettle grows erect to heights of up to 40 cm. The stems are square, and the leaves are opposite and simple, lance-shaped, and hairy. The flowers are pale purple and appear at the top of the spike, often in interrupted fashion.

The genus name, *Stachys*, is Greek for "spike," referring to the inflorescence type. The species name, *palustris*, is Latin meaning "of wet places," and *pilosa* refers to the fine hairs on the leaves and stems of the plant.

Marsh Scullcap
Scutellaria galericulata L.

MINT FAMILY

This member of the Mint family grows to heights of 80 cm at low to mid elevations in wetlands, along lakeshores, on streambanks, and in ditches. The leaves are opposite, oval to lance-shaped, and irregularly scalloped along the blades. The stem is square, typical of the Mint family. The trumpet-shaped flowers have a hooded upper lip and a broad, hairless lower lip, and are blue to purplish-pink, marked with white. The flowers occur as solitary on slender stalks or as pairs in the leaf axils.

The common name for the plant comes from the hood-like appearance of the upper lip of the flower. The species name, *galericulata*, means "helmet-shaped." The plant contains a flavonoid called scutellaria that has sedative and anti-spasmodic properties. A tea made from the plant has long been used by herbalists to treat nervous disorders.

Wild Mint (Canada Mint)

Mentha arvensus L. (ALSO *Mentha canadensis* L.)

MINT FAMILY

This plant inhabits wetland marshes, moist woods, and banks and shores of streams and lakes, and sometimes lives in shallow water. The purplish to pinkish to bluish flowers are crowded in dense clusters in the upper leaf axils. The leaves are opposite, prominently veined, and highly scented of mint if crushed. The stems are square in cross section and hairy.

The genus name, *Mentha*, is derived from the Greek *Minthe*, a mythological nymph loved by Pluto. A jealous Proserpine changed the nymph into a mint plant. The species name, *arvensis*, means "growing in fields." The strong, distinctive taste of mint plants comes from their volatile oils. The leaves have long been used fresh, dried, and frozen as a flavouring and for teas. Some Native peoples used the leaves to flavour meat and pemmican, and lined dried meat containers with mint leaves prior to winter storage. Strong mint teas were used by Native peoples and European settlers as a treatment for coughs, colds, and fevers.

Alfalfa
Medicago sativa L.

PEA FAMILY

Alfalfa is an introduced species that was brought to North America as a forage crop for livestock. It has escaped from cultivated fields and is now locally common in roadside ditches and rights of way. The leaves are elliptic to oblong and occur in threes. They are slightly hairy and sharply toothed at the tips. The flowers are pea-like and purple to blue, occurring in oblong clusters. The fruits are spirally coiled pods.

Alfalfa is said to have been cultivated as far back in history as the Medes in ancient Persia. The Greeks introduced the plant to Europe at the time of the Persian wars. Black Medick (*M. lupulina*) is a close relative of Alfalfa found in the same habitat. Black Medick has yellow flowers, and its fruit is less tightly coiled than Alfalfa"s and turns black at maturity. Alfalfa is similar to another common introduced species, Sweet-Clover (*Melilotus* spp.), but Alfalfa generally has narrower and more wedge-shaped leaves that are toothed only near the tip.

Showy Locoweed
Oxytropis splendens DOUGL.

PEA FAMILY

This attractive member of the pea family has silvery leaves growing from a branched, woody stock. The flower stalk is elongated and holds dense clusters of numerous flowers above the silvery leaves. The flowers are purple to bluish and shaped like other members of the pea family.

Locoweeds are poisonous to cattle, horses, and sheep because the plants contain an alkaloid that can cause blind staggering, thus the common name. The genus name, *Oxytropis*, comes from the Greek *oxys*, meaning "sharp," and *tropis*, meaning "keel," a reference to the flower shape.

Silky Lupine
Lupinus sericeus PURSH

PEA FAMILY

A leafy, erect, tufted perennial with stout stems that appears in sandy to gravelly grasslands, open woods, and roadsides, often growing in dense clumps or bunches. The plant can reach heights of up to 80 cm. The flowers are showy, in dense, long, terminal clusters, and display a variety of colours in blues and purples, occasionally white and yellow. Tremendous colour variation can occur, even in plants that are very close to each other. Flowers have a typical pea shape, with a strongly truncated keel and a pointed tip. The leaves of Lupines are very distinctive. They are palmately compound and alternate on the stem, with five to nine very narrow leaflets that have silky hairs on both sides.

The genus name, *Lupinus*, is from the Latin *lupus*, meaning "wolf." That much appears to be accepted, but how this name came to be applied to this plant is open to contention. Perhaps the best explanation is that the plants were once thought (inaccurately) to be a devourer or robber of soil nutrients, hence a wolf. In fact, the root nodules of Lupines produce a nitrogen-fixing bacterium that actually tends to enrich poor soil. The species name, *sericeus*, is from the Latin *sericus*, meaning "silk," a reference to the soft, silky hairs that cover the plant. The fruits of Lupine contain an alkaloid and may be poisonous to some livestock, particularly sheep.

Timber Milk-Vetch
Astragalus miser DOUGL.

PEA FAMILY

This plant is often widespread and common at low to mid elevations in open Ponderosa pine and Douglas Fir forests. It grows from a taproot and can reach heights of 40 cm, with both prostrate and erect stems. The leaves are pinnately compound (like a feather) with seven to 21 very thin, almost needle-like leaflets. The end leaflet is usually longer than the adjacent pair. The flowers are pea-like and vary in colour from white to pale violet, usually with blue pencilling. The flowers occur in loose, elongated clusters of seven to 20 flowers. The fruits are thin, stalkless, drooping pods, hanging from the flowering stalk.

Timber Milk-Vetch is considered poisonous, particularly to cattle. Some soils derived from shale contain high concentrations of the element selenium, and some members of this genus will take up this element and store it. If a grazing animal eats such plants, it often evinces symptoms of the blind staggers, similar to Locoweed (*Oxytropis* ssp.).

Wild Vetch

Vicia americana L.

PEA FAMILY

This plant thrives in shady riverine habitats, open woods, thickets, and meadows. The purple flowers are typical of the pea family. The leaves are alternate and pinnate, and have forked tendrils at the ends of the leaves. The plant creeps and climbs over adjacent plants.

The genus name, *Vicia*, is from the Latin *vincio*, meaning "to bind together," referring to the binding tendrils on the leaves. *Vicia* was apparently translated to Old North French as *veche* and later became the English word "vetch." Vetches can build nitrates in soil and are looked upon as good forage for livestock.

Shooting Star
Dodecatheon pulchellum (RAF.) MERR.

PRIMROSE FAMILY

This beautiful plant is scattered and locally common at low to alpine elevations in warm, dry climates, grasslands, mountain meadows, and streambanks. The leaves appear in a basal rosette, lance- to spatula-shaped. The flowers appear, one to several, nodding atop a leafless stalk. The flowers are purple to lavender, occasionally white, with corolla lobes turned backwards. The stamens are united into a yellow to orange tube, from which the style and anthers protrude.

A harbinger of spring, these lovely flowers bloom in huge numbers, and the prairies take on a purple hue when the Shooting Stars are in bloom. The genus name, *Dodecatheon*, is from the Greek *dodeka*, meaning "twelve," and *theos*, meaning "gods," thus a plant that is protected by twelve gods. The species name, *pulchellum*, is Latin for "beautiful." Native peoples used an infusion from this plant as an eyewash, and some looked upon the plant as a charm to obtain wealth. Some tribes mashed the flowers to make a pink dye for their arrows. The common name is an apt description of the flower, with the turned-back petals streaming behind the stamens.

Marsh Cinquefoil
Potentilla palustris (L.) SCOP.

ROSE FAMILY

This plant inhabits bogs, marshes, streams, and ponds from the valleys to the subalpine zone. It grows from long, smooth rhizomes, creeping along the ground and rooting at the nodes. The leaves are usually smooth and pinnately compound, with five to seven obovate (teardrop shaped) leaflets that are deeply toothed. While other members of the *Potentilla* family have yellow or white/cream-coloured flowers, Marsh Cinquefoil has purple to deep red flowers.

The species name, *palustris,* is from the Latin *palus* or *palud* and means "marsh" or "swamp," a reference to the favoured habitat of the plant. The flowers have an offensive, rotten odour that attracts insects as pollinators.

Bog Violet
Viola nephrophylla L.

VIOLET FAMILY

A beautiful, small violet that grows in moist meadows, streambanks, and woods. The leaves and flower stalks arise from the base of the plant. The leaves are oval- to kidney-shaped, smooth, and scalloped on the margins. The purple to blue flowers each have a spur 2–3 mm long.

Violets are high in vitamins C and A, and have been used as food back to early Greek and Roman times. They are still cultivated for that purpose in some parts of Europe. The young leaves and flower buds may be used in salads or boiled.

Early Blue Violet
Viola adunca SM.

VIOLET FAMILY

A plant of the grasslands and open woods and slopes. The flower has purple and white petals with darker guidelines. The largest petal has a hooked spur half as long as the lower petal. Side petals are white-bearded. The leaves are mostly basal, oval with a heart-shaped base, and the margins have round teeth. The plant grows low to the ground.

Viola is from the Latin *violaceous*, for the purple colour. *Adunca* means "hooked," a reference to the hook on the spur of the flower. An uncus was a hook used by the Romans to drag executed bodies away from the place of execution. Violets have been used for food for centuries. The leaves are high in vitamins A and C, and can be used to make a bland tea. Violet seeds have special oily bodies called elaiosomes, which attract ants. The ants carry the seeds away to their nests, thus dispersing the seeds. Common garden Pansies are also a member of the *Viola* family.

Thread-Leaved Phacelia (Thread-Leaved Scorpionweed)
Phacelia linearis (PURSH) HOLZ.

WATERLEAF FAMILY

This plant appears on dry plateaus and foothills in our area, and reaches heights of up to 50 cm. It is an annual species of *Phacelia*. The leaves are hairy, alternate, thin and linear below, developing side lobes higher on the stem. The flowers are reasonably large, lavender to blue, and appearing in open clusters from the leaf axils.

The common name, Scorpionweed, most probably arises because some people say the coiled branches of the flower clusters resemble the tail of a scorpion. The genus name, *Phacelia*, is from the Greek *phakelos*, meaning "bundle" or "cluster," a reference to the tightly clustered appearance of the flowers on some members of the genus. The first specimen of the species was collected by Meriwether Lewis in the spring of 1806 near The Dalles, Oregon.

GLOSSARY

Achene: A dry, single-seeded fruit that does not split open at maturity

Alternate: A reference to the arrangement of leaves on a stem where the leaves appear singly and staggered on opposite sides of the stem

Anther: The portion of the stamen (the male portion of a flower) that produces pollen

Axil: The upper angle formed where a leaf, branch, or other organ is attached to a plant stem

Basal: A reference to leaves where the leaves are found at the base or bottom of the plant, usually near ground level

Bract: A reduced or otherwise modified leaf that is usually found near the flower or inflorescence of a plant, but is not part of the flower or inflorescence

Calyx: The outer set of flower parts, usually composed of sepals

Corolla: The collective term for the petals of the flower that are found inside the sepals

Disk flower: Any of the small, tubular florets found in the central clustered portion of the flower head of members of the Composite Family; also referred to as "disk florets"

Drupe: A fleshy or juicy fruit that covers a single, stony seed inside, e.g., a cherry or a peach

Drupelet: Any one part of an aggregate fruit (such as a raspberry or blackberry), where each such part is a fleshy fruit that covers a single, stony seed inside

Florescence: Generally the flowering part of a plant; the arrangement of the flowers on the stem; also referred to as "inflorescence"

Floret: One of the small, tubular flowers in the central, clustered portion of the flower head of members of the Composite Family; also known as, "disk flower"

Gland: A small organ that secrets a sticky or oily substance and is attached to some part of the plant

Glandular hairs: Small hairs attached to glands on plants

Inflorescence: Generally the flowering part of a plant; the arrangement of the flowers on the stem; also referred to as "florescence"

Involucral bract: A modified leaf found just below an inflorescence

Keel: A ridge or fold shaped like the bottom of a boat, which may refer to leaf structure, or more often to the two fused petals in flowers that are members of the Pea Family

Lance-shaped: In reference to leaf shape, much longer than wide, widest below the middle and tapering to the tip, like the blade of a lance

Nectary: A plant structure that produces and secrets nectar

Obovate: Shaped like a teardrop

Opposite: A reference to the arrangement of leaves on a stem where the leaves appear paired on opposite sides of the stem, directly across from each other

Palmate: A reference to the arrangement of leaves on a stem where the leaves spread like the fingers on a hand, diverging from a central or common point

Panicle: A branched inflorescence that blooms from the bottom up

Pappus: The cluster of bristles, scales, or hairs at the top of an achene in the flowers of the Composite Family

Petal: A component of the inner floral portion of a flower, often the most brightly coloured and visible part of the flower

Petiole: The stem of a leaf

Pinnate: A reference to the arrangement of leaves on a stem where the leaves appear in two rows on opposite sides of a central stem, similar to the construction of a feather

Pistil: The female part of a flower; it includes the stigma, style, and ovary

Pome: A fruit with a core, e.g., an apple or pear

Raceme: A flower arrangement that has an elongated flower cluster with the flowers attached to short stalks of relatively equal length; these stalks are attached to the main central stalk

Ray flower: One of the outer, strap-shaped petals seen in members of the Composite Family. Ray flowers may surround disk flowers or may comprise the whole of the flower head

Saprophyte: An organism that obtains its nutrients from dead organic matter

Sepal: A leaf-like appendage that surrounds the petals of a flower. Collectively the sepals make up the calyx

Spur: A hollow, tubular projection arising from the base of a petal or sepal, often producing nectar

Spurred corolla: A corolla that has spurs

Stamen: The male flower part that produces pollen, typically consisting of an anther and a filament

Staminode: A sterile stamen

Standard: The uppermost petal of a typical flower in the Pea Family

Stigma: The pollen-collecting tip of the female part of the flower, the pistil

Stipule: An appendage, usually in pairs, found at the base of a leaf or leaf stalk

Style: A slender stalk connecting the stigma to the ovary in the female organ of a flower

Talus: Loose, fragmented rock rubble usually found at the base of a rock wall, also known as "scree"

Taproot: A stout main root that extends downward

Terminal flower head: A flower that appears at the top of a stem, as opposed to originating from a leaf axil

Ternate: Arranged in threes, often in

reference to leaf structures

Umbel: A flower arrangement where the flower stalks have a common point of attachment to the stem, like the spokes of an umbrella

Vacuole: A membrane-bound compartment in a plant that is typically filled with liquid, and may perform various functions in the plant

Wings: Side petals that flank the keel in typical flowers of the Pea Family

PLANT FAMILIES ARRANGED ACCORDING TO COLOUR

YELLOW FLOWERS

Barberry Family
Oregon Grapes
Borage Family
Puccoon (Lemonweed)
Buckwheat Family
Yellow Buckwheat
(Umbrella Plant)
Buttercup Family
Marsh Marigold
Sagebrush Buttercup
Creeping Buttercup
Meadow Buttercup
Yellow Columbine
Carrot Family
Heart-Leaved Alexander
(Meadow Parsnip)
Narrow-Leaved Desert Parsley
(Nine-Leaf Biscuit-Root)
Composite Family
Annual Hawk's-Beard
Arrow-Leaved Balsamroot
Arrow-Leaved Groundsel
(Giant Ragwort)
Brown-Eyed Susan
Common Dandelion
Common Tansy
Goat's-Beard
Hairy Golden Aster
Heart-Leafed Arnica
Late Goldenrod
Perennial Sow Thistle
Pineapple Weed
Prairie Coneflower
Prairie Groundsel
Prickly Lettuce
Shiny Arnica (Orange Arnica)
Short-Beaked Agoseris (False
Dandelion)
Slender Hawkweed
Spike-Like Goldenrod
Evening Primrose Family

Yellow Evening Primrose
Figwort Family
Butter and Eggs
Mullein
Yellow Beardtongue
(Yellow Penstemon)
Yellow Monkeyflower
Yellow Owl's Clover
Fumitory Family
Golden Corydalis
Honeysuckle Family
Black Twinberry (Bracted
Honeysuckle)
Twining Honeysuckle
Lily Family
Glacier Lily
Yellowbell
Maple Family
Douglas Maple
(Rocky Mountain Maple)
Mustard Family
Prairie Rocket
Flixweed
Oleaster Family
Soopolallie (Canadian
Buffaloberry)
Wolf Willow (Silverberry)
Orchid Family
Pale Coralroot
Yellow Lady's Slipper
Pea Family
Buffalo Bean (Golden Bean)
Field Locoweed
Yellow Hedysarum
Yellow Sweet-Clover
Rose Family
Antelope Brush
(Pursh's Bitterbrush)
Early Cinquefoil
Shrubby Cinquefoil
Sticky Cinquefoil
Yellow Avens
Yellow Mountain Avens

St. John's Wort Family
Common St. John's Wort
Violet Family
Round-Leaved Violet
Yellow Wood Violet

RED, ORANGE, & PINK FLOWERS

Bittersweet Family
Falsebox
Buttercup Family
Red Columbine
Western Meadow Rue
Wind Flower
Composite Family
Orange Hawkweed
Pink Pussytoes (Rosy Pussytoes)
Spotted Knapweed
Currant Family
Black Gooseberry
(Swamp Currant)
Dogbane Family
Spreading Dogbane
Evening Primrose Family
Fireweed
River Beauty
Scarlet Butterflyweed
Figwort Family
Elephant's Head
Paintbrush
Thin-Leaved Owl's Clover
Goosefoot Family
Strawberry Blite
Heath Family
False Azalea
(Fool's Huckleberry)
Grouseberry
Huckleberry
Kinnikinnick (Bearberry)
Pine-Drops
Pink Wintergreen
Prince's-Pine (Pipsissewa)
Western Bog-Laurel
(Swamp Laurel)
Honeysuckle Family
Twinflower

Lily Family
Nodding Onion
Sagebrush mariposa Lily
Tiger Lily
Western Wood Lily
Mint Family
Wild Bergamot
Orchid Family
Spotted Coralroot
Striped Coralroot
Venus's Slipper
Pea Family
Red Clover
Purslane Family
Bitterroot
Rose Family
Old Man's Whiskers
(Three Flowered Avens)
Prickly Rose

WHITE, GREEN, & BROWN FLOWERS

Birch Family
Sitka Alder
Buckthorn Family
Buckbrush Ceanothus
(Snowbrush)
Buttercup Family
Baneberry
Canada Anemone
Northern Anemone
Carrot Family
Cow Parsnip
Large-Fruited Desert-Parsley
Sharptooth Angelica
(Lyall's Angelica)
Water Hemlock
Cattail Family
Common Cattail
Composite Family
Broad-Leaved Pussytoes
(Broad-Leaved Everlasting)
Ox-Eye Daisy
Pearly Everlasting
Small-Leaved Everlasting
Tufted Fleabane

White Hawkweed
Yarrow
Currant Family
    Northern Black Currant
      (Skunk Currant)
    Sticky Currant
Dogwood Family
    Bunchberry (Dwarf Dogwood)
    Red Osier Dogwood
Figwort Family
    Eyebright
    Parrot's Beak
Geranium Family
    White Geranium
Ginseng Family
    Devil's Club
    Wild Sarsaparilla
Grass-of-Parnassus Family
    Fringed Grass of Parnassus
Heath Family
    Greenish Flowered Wintergreen
    Labrador Tea
    One-Sided Wintergreen
    Oval-Leaved Blueberry
    Painted Pyrola
      (White-Veined Wintergreen)
    Single Delight
    Western Mountain Heather
    White Rhododendron
Honeysuckle Family
    Black Elderberry
    Blue Elderberry
    Snowberry
    Utah Honeysuckle
      (Red Twinberry)
Lily Family
    Bronzebells
    Clasping-Leaved Twisted-Stalk
    Death Camas
    Fairybells
    False Solomon's Seal
    Indian Hellebore
    Queen's Cup
    Star Flowered Solomon's Seal
    Sticky False Asphodel

Three Spot Mariposa Lily
White Camas
Yucca
Madder Family
    Northern Bedstraw
Morning Glory Family
    Morning Glory
Mustard Family
    Reflexed Rock Cress
Nettle Family
    Stinging Nettle
Nightshade Family
    Black Henbane
Orchid Family
    Blunt-Leaved Bog Orchid
    Heart-Leaved Twayblade
    Hooded Ladies' Tresses
    Rattlesnake Plantain
    Round-Leaved Orchid
    Tall White Bog Orchid
Pea Family
    White Clover (Dutch Clover)
    White Peavine
Phlox Family
    Moss Phlox
Pink Family
    Bladder Campion
    Field Chickweed
      (Mouse-Ear Chickweed)
Primrose Family
    Mealy Primrose
    Starflower
    Sweet-Flowered Androsace
      (Rock Jasmine)
Purslane Family
    Western Spring Beauty
Rose Family
    Birch-Leaf Spirea
    Black Hawthorn
    Chokecherry
    Saskatoon (Serviceberry)
    Thimbleberry
    Trailing Raspberry
    Western Mountain Ash
    White Cinquefoil

Wild Red Raspberry
Wild Strawberry
Sandalwood Family
Pale Comandra
(Bastard Toadflax)
Saxifrage Family
Foamflower
Small-Flowered Woodland Star
Round-Leaved Alumroot
Spotted Saxifrage
Valerian Family
Sitka Valerian
Violet Family
Western Canada Violet

BLUE & PURPLE FLOWERS

Borage Family
Common Hound's-Tongue
Forget-Me-Not
Mertensia (Low Lungwort)
Blueweed
Western Stickseed
Buttercup Family
Blue Clematis
Blue Columbine
Low Larkspur
Monkshood
Prairie Crocus
Carrot Family
Fern-Leaved Desert Parsley
Composite Family
Blue Lettuce (Horseweed)
Blue Sailor
Bull Thistle
Canada Thistle
Common Burdock
Showy Aster
Smooth Blue Aster
Figwort Family
Blue-Eyed Mary

Creeping Beardtongue
Shrubby Penstemon
Small-Flowered Penstemon
(Small Flowered
Beardtongue)
Taper-Leaved Beardtongue
Flax Family
Blue Flax
Gentian Family
Northern Gentian
Geranium Family
Sticky Purple Geranium
Harebell Family
Harebell
Iris Family
Blue-Eyed Gras
Lily Family
Wild Chives
Mint Family
Giant Hyssop
Heal-All
Marsh Hedge-Nettle
Marsh Scullcap
Wild Mint (Canada Mint)
Pea Family
Alfalfa
Showy Locoweed
Silky Lupine
Timber Milk-Vetch
Wild Vetch
Primrose Family
Shooting Star
Rose Family
Marsh Cinquefoil
Violet Family
Bog Violet
Early Blue Violet
Waterleaf Family
Thread-Leaved Phacelia
(Thread-Leaved Scorpionweed)

Bibliography

Clark, L.J. and J. Trelawny (ed.), 1973, 1976, 1998. *Wildflowers of the Pacific Northwest.* Harbour Publishing, Madeira Park, British Columbia.

Cormack, R.G.H., 1977. *Wild Flowers of Alberta.* Hurtig Publishers, Edmonton, Alberta.

Kershaw, L., A. MacKinnon, and J. Polar, 1998. *Plants of the Rocky Mountains.* Lone Pine Publishing, Edmonton, Alberta.

Parish, R., R. Coupe, and D. Lloyd (ed.), 1996. *Plants of Southern Interior British Columbia.* Lone Pine Publishing, Edmonton, Alberta.

Phillips, W.H., 2001. *Northern Rocky Mountain Wildflowers.* Falcon, Helena, Montana.

Scotter, G.W., and H. Flygare, 1986. *Wildflowers of the Canadian Rockies.* Hurtig Publishers Ltd., Toronto, Ontario.

Vance, F.R., J.R. Jowsey, J.S. McLean, and F.A. Switzer, 1999. *Wildflowers Across the Prairies.* Greystone Books, Vancouver, British Columbia.

Wilkinson, K., 1999. *Wildflowers of Alberta.* The University of Alberta Press and Lone Pine Publishing, Edmonton, Alberta.

Index

240